hamlyn | **all colour cookbook**

200 Light
slow cooker

An Hachette UK Company
www.hachette.co.uk

First published in Great Britain in 2015 by Hamlyn
a division of Octopus Publishing Group Ltd, Carmelite
House, 50 Victoria Embankment, London, EC4Y 0DZ
www.octopusbooks.co.uk

ISBN: 978-0-600-62906-1
A CIP catalogue record for this book is available
from the British Library.

Printed and bound in China

10 9 8 7 6 5 4 3 2

Both metric and imperial measurements have been given
in all recipes. Use one set of measurements only, and not a
mixture of both.

Standard level spoon measurements are used in all recipes.
1 tablespoon = one 15 ml spoon
1 teaspoon = one 5 ml spoon

Ovens should be preheated to the specified temperature
– if using a fan-assisted oven, follow the manufacturer's
instructions for adjusting the time and temperature.

Fresh herbs and medium eggs should be used unless
otherwise stated.

The Department of Health advises that eggs should not
be consumed raw. This book contains some dishes made
with raw or lightly cooked eggs. It is prudent for vulnerable
people such as pregnant and nusing mothers, invalids,
the elderly, babies and young children to avoid uncooked
or lightly cooked dishes made with eggs. Once prepared,
these dishes should be kept refrigerated and used promptly.

This book includes dishes made with nuts and nut
derivatives. It is advisable for those with known allergic
reactions to nuts and nut derivatives and those who may
be potentially vulnerable to these allergies to avoid dishes
made with nuts and nut oils. It is also prudent to check the
labels of pre-prepared ingredients for the possible inclusion
of nut derivatives.

200 Light
slow cooker

contents

introduction

introduction

this series

The Hamlyn All Colour Light Series is a collection of handy-sized books, each packed with over 200 healthy recipes on a variety of topics and cuisines to suit your needs.

The books are designed to help those people who are trying to lose weight by offering a range of delicious recipes that are low in calories but still high in flavour. The recipes show a calorie count per portion, so you will know exactly what you are eating. These are recipes for real and delicious food, not ultra-slimming meals, so they will help you maintain a new healthier eating plan for life. They must be used as part of a balanced diet, with the cakes and sweet dishes eaten only as an occasional treat.

how to use this book

All the recipes in this book are clearly marked with the number of calories (kcal) per serving. The chapters cover different calorie bands: under 500, 400, 300 and 200 calories. There are variations on each recipe at the bottom of the page – note the variation calorie counts as they do vary and can sometimes be more than the original recipe.

The figures assume that you are using low-fat versions of dairy products, so be sure to use skimmed milk and low-fat yogurt. They have also been calculated using lean meat, so make sure you trim meat of all visible fat and remove the skin from chicken breasts.

Use moderate amounts of oil and butter for cooking and low-fat/low-calorie alternatives when you can.

Don't forget to note the number of portions each recipe makes and divide up the food accordingly, so that you know how many calories you are consuming. Be careful about side dishes and accompaniments that will add to calorie content.

Above all, enjoy trying out the new flavours and exciting recipes that this book contains. Rather than dwelling on the thought that you are denying yourself your usual unhealthy treats, think of your new regime as a positive step towards a new you. Not only will you lose weight and feel more confident, but your health will benefit, the condition of your hair and nails will improve, and you will take on a healthy glow.

the risks of obesity

Up to half of women and two-thirds of men are overweight or obese in the developed world today. Being overweight can not only make us unhappy with our appearance, but can also lead to serious health problems.

When someone is obese, it means they are overweight to the point that it could start to seriously threaten their health. In fact, obesity ranks as a close second to smoking as a possible cause of cancer. Obese women are more likely to have complications during and after pregnancy, and people who are overweight or obese are also more likely to suffer from coronary heart disease, gallstones, osteoarthritis, high blood pressure and type 2 diabetes.

how can I tell if I am overweight?

The best way to tell if you are overweight is to work out your body mass index (BMI). If using metric measurements, divide your weight in kilograms (kg) by your height in metres (m) squared. (For example, if you are 1.7 m tall and weigh 70 kg, the calculation would be 70 ÷ 2.89 = 24.2.) If using imperial measurements, divide your weight in pounds (lb) by your height in inches (in) squared and multiply by 703. Then compare the figure to the list right (these figures apply to healthy adults only).

Less than 20	underweight
20–25	healthy
25–30	overweight
Over 30	obese

As we all know by now, one of the major causes of obesity is eating too many calories.

what is a calorie?

Our bodies need energy to stay alive, grow, keep warm and be active. We get the energy we need to survive from the food and drinks we consume – more specifically, from the fat, carbohydrate, protein and alcohol that they contain.

A calorie (cal), as anyone who has ever been on a diet will know, is the unit used to measure how much energy different foods contain. A calorie can be scientifically defined as the energy required to raise the temperature of 1 gram of water from 14.5°C to 15.5°C. A kilocalorie (kcal) is 1,000 calories and it is, in fact, kilocalories that we usually mean when we talk about the calories in different foods.

Different food types contain different numbers of calories. For example, a gram of carbohydrate (starch or sugar) provides 3.75 kcal, protein provides 4 kcal per gram, fat provides 9 kcal per gram and alcohol provides 7 kcal per gram. So, fat is the most concentrated source of energy – weight for weight, it provides just over twice as many calories as either protein or carbohydrate

– with alcohol not far behind. The energy content of a food or drink depends on how many grams of carbohydrate, fat, protein and alcohol are present.

how many calories do we need?

The number of calories we need to consume varies from person to person, but your body weight is a clear indication of whether you are eating the right amount. Body weight is simply determined by the number of calories you are eating compared to the number of calories your body is using to maintain itself and is needed for physical activity. If you regularly consume more calories than you use up, you will start to gain weight as extra energy is stored in the body as fat.

Based on our relatively inactive modern-day lifestyles, most nutritionists recommend that women should aim to consume around 2,000 calories (kcal) per day, and men an amount of around 2,500. Of course, the amount of energy required depends on your level of activity: the more active you are, the more energy you need to maintain a stable weight.

a healthier lifestyle

To maintain a healthy body weight, we need to expend as much energy as we eat; to lose weight, energy expenditure must therefore exceed intake of calories. So, exercise is a vital tool in the fight to lose weight. Physical activity doesn't just help us control body weight; it also helps to reduce our appetite and is known to have beneficial effects on the heart and blood that help guard against cardiovascular disease.

Many of us claim we don't enjoy exercise and simply don't have the time to fit it into our hectic schedules. So the easiest way to increase physical activity is by incorporating it into our daily routines, perhaps by walking or cycling instead of driving (particularly for short journeys), taking up more active hobbies such as gardening, and taking small and simple steps, such as using the stairs instead of the lift whenever possible.

As a general guide, adults should aim to undertake at least 30 minutes of moderate-intensity exercise, such as a brisk walk, five times a week. The 30 minutes does not have to be taken all at once: three sessions of 10 minutes are equally beneficial. Children and young people should be encouraged to take at least 60 minutes of moderate-intensity exercise every day.

Some activities will use up more energy than others. The following list shows some examples of the energy a person weighing 60 kg (132 lb) would expend doing the following activities for 30 minutes:

activity	energy
Ironing	69 kcal
Cleaning	75 kcal
Walking	99 kcal
Golf	129 kcal
Fast walking	150 kcal
Cycling	180 kcal
Aerobics	195 kcal
Swimming	195 kcal
Running	300 kcal
Sprinting	405 kcal

make changes for life

The best way to lose weight is to try to adopt healthier eating habits that you can easily maintain all the time, not just when you are trying to slim down. Aim to lose no more than 1 kg (2 lb) per week to ensure you lose only your fat stores. People who go on crash diets lose lean muscle as well as fat and are much more likely to put the weight back on again soon afterwards.

For a woman, the aim is to reduce her daily calorie intake to around 1,500 kcal while she is trying to lose weight, then settle on around 2,000 per day thereafter to maintain her new body weight. A regime of regular exercise will also make a huge difference: the more you

can burn, the less you will need to limit your food intake.

improve your diet

For most of us, simply adopting a more balanced diet will reduce our calorie intake and lead to weight loss. Follow these simple recommendations:

- Eat more starchy foods, such as bread, potatoes, rice and pasta. Assuming these replace the fattier foods you usually eat, and you don't smother them with oil or butter, this will help reduce the amount of fat and increase the amount of fibre in your diet.
- Try to use wholegrain rice, pasta and flour, as the energy from these foods is released more slowly in the body, making you feel fuller for longer.

- Eat more fruit and vegetables, aiming for at least five portions of different fruit and vegetables a day (excluding potatoes).
- Eat fewer sugary foods, such as biscuits, cakes and chocolate bars. This will also help reduce your fat intake. If you fancy something sweet, choose fresh or dried fruit instead.
- Reduce the amount of fat in your diet, so you consume fewer calories. Choosing low-fat versions of dairy products, such as skimmed milk and low-fat yogurt, doesn't necessarily mean your food will be tasteless. Low-fat versions are available for most dairy products, including milk, cheese, crème fraîche, yogurt, and even cream and butter.
- Choose lean cuts of meat, such as back bacon instead of streaky, and chicken breasts instead of thighs. Trim all visible fat off meat before cooking and avoid frying foods – grill or roast them instead. Fish is also naturally low in fat and can make a variety of tempting dishes.

As long as you don't add extra fat to your fruit and vegetables in the form of cream, butter or oil, these changes will help reduce your fat intake and increase the amount of fibre and vitamins you consume.

simple steps to reduce your intake

Few of us have an iron will, so when you are trying to cut down make it easier on yourself by following these steps:

- Serve small portions to start with. You may feel satisfied when you have finished, but if you are still hungry you can always go back for more.
- Once you have served up your meal, put away any leftover food before you eat. Don't put heaped serving dishes on the table as you will undoubtedly pick, even if you feel satisfied with what you have already eaten.
- Eat slowly and savour your food; then you are more likely to feel full when you have finished. If you rush a meal, you may still feel hungry afterwards.
- Make an effort with your meals. Just because you are cutting down doesn't mean your meals have to be low on taste as well as calories. You will feel more satisfied with a meal you have really enjoyed and will be less likely to look for comfort in a bag of crisps or a bar of chocolate.
- Plan your meals in advance to make sure you have all the ingredients you need. Casting around in the cupboards when you are hungry is unlikely to result in a healthy, balanced meal.
- Keep healthy and interesting snacks to hand for those moments when you need something to pep you up. You don't need to succumb to a chocolate bar if there are other tempting, but healthy, treats on offer.

slow cooking

If you want to prepare healthy, homely meals but feel you just don't have time, then think again. As little as 15—20 minutes spent early in the day is all that is needed to prepare supper to go into a slow cooker, leaving you free to get on with something else.

Because the food cooks so slowly there is no need to worry about it boiling dry, spilling over or burning on the bottom. Depending on the setting it can be left for 8—10 hours. Slow-cooked food often has much more flavour than dishes prepared in other ways.

When water is added to the pot of a slow cooker it can be used as a *bain marie* (water bath) to cook baked custards, pâtés or terrines. Alcoholic or fruit juice mixtures can be poured into the pot to make warming party punches or hot toddies. Slow cookers are perfect for steaming puddings, too. Because there is no evaporation you won't have to top up the water or return to find that the pot has boiled dry. The slow cooker pot can also be used to make chocolate or cheese fondues, preserves such as lemon curd or simple chutneys, and you can boil up bones or a chicken carcass for homemade stock.

size matters

Unless you have a large family, or like to cook large quantities so that you have enough supper for one meal with extra portions to freeze, you will probably find a slow cooker too big for your everyday needs. Remember that you need to at least half-fill a slow cooker when you are cooking meat, fish or vegetable dishes.

Slow cookers are available in three sizes and are measured in capacity. The size usually printed on the packaging is the working capacity or the maximum space for food:

- For two people, use a mini oval slow cooker with a maximum capacity of 1.5 litres (2½ pints) and a working capacity of 1 litre (1¾ pints).
- For four people, choose a round or more versatile oval cooker with a maximum capacity of 3.5 litres (6 pints) and a working capacity of 2.5 litres (4 pints).
- For six people, you will need a large oval slow cooker with a maximum capacity of 5 litres (8¾ pints) and a working capacity of 4 litres (7 pints), or an extra large round cooker

how full should the pot be?

A slow cooker pot must only be used with the addition of liquid – ideally it should be no less than half full. Aim for the three-quarter full mark or, if you are making soups, make sure the liquid is no higher than 2.5 cm (1 inch) from the top. Joints of meat should take up no more than two-thirds of the pot. If you are using a pudding basin, ensure there is 1.5 cm (¾ inch) space all the way round or 1 cm (½ inch) at the narrowest point for an oval cooker.

heat settings

All slow cookers have a 'high', 'low' and 'off' setting, and some also have 'medium', 'warm' or 'auto' settings. In general, the 'high' setting will take only half the time of the 'low' setting when you are cooking a diced meat or vegetable casserole. This can be useful if you plan to eat at lunchtime or are delayed in starting the casserole. Both settings will reach just below 100°C (212°F), boiling point, during cooking, but when it is set to 'high' the temperature is reached more quickly. A combination of settings can be useful and is recommended by some manufacturers at the beginning of cooking. (See your manufacturer's handbook for more details.) The following is a general guide to what you should cook at which temperature.

with a maximum capacity of 6.5 litres (11½ pints) and a working capacity of 4.5 litres (8 pints).

The best and most versatile shape for a slow cooker is an oval, which is ideal for cooking a whole chicken and has ample room for a pudding basin or four individual pudding moulds and yet is capacious enough to make soup for six. Choose one with an indicator light so that you can see at a glance when the slow cooker is turned on.

before you start

It is important to read the manufacturer's handbook before using your slow cooker. Some recommend preheating the slow cooker on High for a minimum of 20 minutes before food is added. Others recommend that it is heated only when filled with food.

low
• Diced meat or vegetable casseroles
• Chops or chicken joints

- Soups
- Egg custard desserts
- Rice dishes
- Fish dishes

high
- Sweet or savoury steamed puddings or sweet dishes that include a raising agent (either self-raising flour or baking powder)
- Pâtés or terrines
- Whole chicken, guinea fowl or pheasant, gammon joint or half a shoulder of lamb.

timings

All the recipes in this book have variable timings, which means that they will be tender and ready to eat at the shorter time but can be left without spoiling for an extra hour or two, which is perfect if you get delayed at work or stuck in traffic. Do not change timings or slow settings for fish, whole joints or dairy dishes. If you want to speed up or slow down diced meat or vegetable casseroles, so that the cooking fits around your plans, adjust the heat settings and timings as follows:

Low	Medium	High
6–8 hours	4–6 hours	3–4 hours
8–10 hours	6–8 hours	5–6 hours
10–12 hours	8–10 hours	7–8 hours

(These timings were taken from the Morphy Richards cooker instruction manual.)

Be aware that as the slow cooker heats up, it forms a water seal just under the lid, but whenever you lift the lid you break the seal. For each time you lift the lid, add 20 minutes to the cooking time. Any pre-cooking is included in the prepararion time.

using your slow cooker for the first time

- Before you start to use the slow cooker, put it on the work surface, somewhere out of the way and make sure that the flex is tucked around the back of the machine and not trailing over the front of the work surface.
- The outside of the slow cooker does get hot, so warn young members of the family.
- Don't forget to wear oven gloves or use tea towels when you are lifting the pot out of the housing, and always place the pot on

a heatproof mat on the table or work surface to serve the food.

- Don't put your slow cooker under an eye-level cupboard if the lid has a vent in the top. The steam from the vent could burn someone's arm as they reach into the cupboard.
- Always check that the joint, pudding basin, soufflé dish or individual moulds will fit into your slow cooker pot before you begin work on a recipe to avoid frustration when you get to a critical point.

preparing food for the slow cooker

Meat: Cut meat into pieces that are the same size so cooking is even, and fry off meat before adding to the slow cooker. A whole guinea fowl or pheasant, a small gammon joint or half a shoulder of lamb can be cooked in an oval slow cooker pot, but make sure that it does not fill more than the lower two-thirds of the pot. Cover the meat with boiling liquid and cook on high. Check it is cooked either by using a meat thermometer or by inserting a skewer through the thickest part and ensuring that the juices run clear. Add boiling stock or sauce to the slow cooker pot and press the meat beneath the surface before cooking begins.

Vegetables: Root vegetables can (surprisingly) take longer to cook than meat. If you are adding vegetables to a meat casserole, make sure you cut them into pieces that are a little

smaller than the meat and try to keep all the vegetable chunks the same size so that they cook evenly. Press the vegetables and the meat below the surface of the liquid before cooking begins. When you are making soup, purée it while it is still in the slow cooker pot, using an electric stick blender if you have one.

Fish: Whether you cut the fish into pieces or cook it in a larger piece of about 500 g (1 lb), the slow, gentle cooking will not cause the fish to break up or overcook. Always make sure that the fish is covered by the hot liquid so that it cooks evenly right through to the centre and do not add shellfish until the last 15 minutes of cooking, when the slow cooker should be set to high. Any frozen fish must be thoroughly thawed, rinsed with cold water and drained before use.

Pasta: For best results, cook the pasta separately in a saucepan of boiling water and then mix with the casserole just before serving. Small pasta shapes, such as macaroni or shells, can be added to soups 30—45 minutes before the end of cooking. Pasta can be soaked in boiling water for 10 minutes prior to adding to short-cook recipes.

Rice: Easy-cook rice is preferable for slow cookers because it has been partially cooked during manufacture and some of the starch has been washed off, making it less sticky. When you are cooking rice, allow a minimum of 250 ml (8 fl oz) water for each 100 g (3½ oz) of easy-cook rice, or up to 500 ml (17 fl oz) for risotto rice.

Dried pulses: Make sure that you soak dried pulses in plenty of cold water overnight. Drain them, then put them into a saucepan with fresh water and bring to the boil. Boil rapidly for 10 minutes, skim off any foam, then drain or add with the cooking liquid to the slow cooker. (See recipes for details.)

changing recipes to suit a different model

All the recipes in this book have been tested in a standard-sized slow cooker for four people with a maximum capacity of 3.5 litres (6 pints). You might have a larger 5 litre (8¾ pint) six-portion sized cooker or a smaller 1.5 litre (2½ pint) two-portion cooker. To adapt the recipes in this book you can simply halve for two portions or add half as much again to the recipe for more portions, keeping the timings the same. All those recipes made in a pudding basin, soufflé dish or individual moulds may also be cooked in a larger slow cooker for the same amount of time.

caring for your slow cooker

If you look after it carefully you may find that your machine lasts for 20 years or more.

Because the heat of a slow cooker is so controllable it is not like a saucepan with burned-on grime to contend with. Once cool, simply lift the slow cooker pot out of the housing, fill the pot with hot, soapy water and leave to soak for a while. Although it is tempting to pop the slow cooker pot and lid into the dishwasher, they do take up a lot of space and not all are dishwasher proof (check your manual).

Allow the machine itself to cool down before cleaning. Turn it off at the controls and pull out the plug. Wipe the inside with a damp cloth, removing any stubborn marks with a little cream cleaner. The outside of the machine and the controls can be wiped with a cloth, then buffed up with a duster or, if it has a chrome-effect finish, sprayed with a little multi-surface cleaner and polished with a duster. Never immerse the machine in water to clean it and if you are storing the slow cooker in a cupboard, make sure it is completely cold before you put it away.

recipes
under 200
calories

breakfast baked tomatoes

Calories per serving **121**
Serves **4**
Preparation time **10 minutes**
Cooking time **8–10 hours**

500 g (1 lb) **plum tomatoes**,
   halved lengthways
leaves from 2–3 **thyme sprigs**
1 tablespoon **balsamic
   vinegar**
salt and **pepper**
chopped **parsley**, to garnish
4 slices of **wholewheat bread**,
   40 g (1½ oz) each, to serve

Preheat the slow cooker if necessary. Arrange the tomatoes, cut sides up, in the slow cooker pot, packing them in tightly in a single layer. Sprinkle with the thyme, drizzle with the vinegar and season to taste. Cover and cook on Low for 8–10 hours overnight.

Toast the bread the next morning and place on 4 serving plates. Top with the tomatoes and a little of the juice and serve sprinkled with parsley.

For balsamic tomatoes with spaghetti, follow the recipe above to cook the tomatoes, then chop them and mix with the cooking juices. Cook 200 g (7 oz) dried spaghetti according to packet instructions, then drain and toss with the tomatoes. Sprinkle each portion with 1 tablespoon grated Parmesan cheese. **Calories per serving 242**

tomato, pepper & garlic bruschetta

Calories per serving **197**
Serves **4**
Preparation time **20 minutes**
Cooking time **3–5 hours**

1 large **red pepper**, quartered,
    cored and deseeded
500 g (1 lb) **plum tomatoes**,
    halved
4 large **garlic cloves**,
    unpeeled
leaves from 2–3 **thyme sprigs**
1 teaspoon **granular**
    sweetener
1 tablespoon **virgin olive oil**
8 slices of **French bread**,
    175 g (6 oz) in total
8 **stoned black olives** in brine,
    drained
salt and **pepper**

Preheat the slow cooker if necessary. Arrange the pepper pieces, skin side down, in the base of the slow cooker pot, arrange the tomatoes on top, then tuck the garlic in among them. Scatter the thyme leaves on top, reserving a little to garnish. Sprinkle with the sweetener and drizzle with the oil.

Season to taste, cover and cook on High for 3–5 hours until the vegetables are tender but the tomatoes still hold their shape.

Lift the vegetables out of the slow cooker pot with a slotted spoon. Peel the skins off the peppers, tomatoes and garlic, then roughly chop the vegetables and toss together. Adjust the seasoning if necessary.

Toast the bread on both sides, arrange on a serving plate, then spoon the tomato mixture on top. Arrange the olives and reserved thyme on the bruschetta and serve as a light lunch or starter.

For quick tomato & pepper pizzas, follow the recipe above to cook the tomato and pepper mixture, then spoon on to 2 halved and toasted ciabatta rolls. Sprinkle with 50 g (2 oz) grated reduced-fat Cheddar cheese and place under a preheated hot grill to melt the cheese. Serve with salad. **Calories per serving 237**

baked peppers with chorizo

Calories per serving **105**
Serves **4**
Preparation time **20 minutes**
Cooking time **3–4 hours**

2 large **red peppers**, halved
  lengthways, cored and
  deseeded
2 **spring onions**, thinly sliced
50 g (2 oz) **chorizo**, finely
  diced
200 g (7 oz) **cherry tomatoes**,
  halved
1–2 **garlic cloves**, finely
  chopped
small handful of **basil**, torn,
  plus extra to garnish
4 pinches of **smoked hot
  paprika**
1 tablespoon **balsamic
  vinegar**
salt and **pepper**

Preheat the slow cooker if necessary. Arrange the peppers, cut sides up, in a single layer in the base of the slow cooker pot. Divide the spring onions and chorizo between the peppers, then pack in the cherry tomatoes.

Sprinkle with the garlic and torn basil, then add a pinch of paprika and a drizzle of balsamic vinegar to each one. Season to taste, cover and cook on High for 3–4 hours until the peppers have softened.

Transfer to a platter and sprinkle with extra basil leaves. Serve hot or cold as a light lunch with salad.

For baked pepper pizzas, follow the recipe above, omitting the chorizo and paprika. When cooked, transfer the peppers to a shallow ovenproof dish. Tear 150 g (5 oz) mozzarella into small pieces, sprinkle over the peppers, then place under a preheated hot grill for 4–5 minutes until the cheese is bubbling and golden. Garnish with extra torn basil and 4 stoned black olives. **Calories per serving 155**

herby stuffed peppers

Calories per serving **190**
Preparation time **20 minutes**
Cooking time **4—5 hours**
Serves **4**

4 **different coloured peppers**
100 g (3½ oz) easy-cook
 brown rice
410 g (13½ oz) can
 chickpeas, drained
small bunch of **parsley**,
 roughly chopped
small bunch of **mint**, roughly
 chopped
1 **onion**, finely chopped
2 **garlic cloves**, finely chopped
½ teaspoon **smoked paprika**
1 teaspoon **ground allspice**
600 ml (1 pint) hot **vegetable
 stock**
salt and **pepper**

Preheat the slow cooker if necessary. Cut the top off
each pepper, then remove the core and seeds.

Mix together the rice, chickpeas, herbs, onion, garlic,
paprika and allspice with plenty of seasoning. Spoon
the mixture into the insides of the peppers, then put the
peppers into the slow cooker pot.

Pour the hot stock around the peppers, cover with the
lid and cook on Low for 4—5 hours or until the rice and
peppers are tender. Spoon into dishes and serve.

For feta-stuffed peppers, make the recipe as above,
but use 100 g (3½ oz) crumbled feta cheese, 40 g
(1½ oz) sultanas, a small bunch of chopped basil and
¼ teaspoon ground allspice instead of the chopped
parsley, mint, paprika and allspice. **Calories per
serving 213**

indian black pepper chicken

Calories per serving **194**
Serves **4**
Preparation time **20 minutes**
Cooking time **7½–8¾ hours**

1 large **onion**, quartered
3 **garlic cloves**, halved
4 cm (1½ inch) piece of **fresh root ginger**, sliced
15 g (½ oz) **fresh coriander**
8 small skinless **chicken drumsticks**, 875 g (1¾ lb) in total
low-calorie cooking oil spray
5 cm (2 inch) **cinnamon stick**
1 teaspoon **ground cumin**
1 teaspoon **ground turmeric**
2 teaspoons **black peppercorns**, roughly crushed
juice of ½ **lemon**
350 ml (12 fl oz) **chicken stock**
150 g (5 oz) **baby spinach**
salt

Preheat the slow cooker if necessary. Place the onion, garlic, ginger and coriander in a food processor and blitz until very finely chopped.

Slash each chicken drumstick 2 or 3 times with a sharp knife. Spray a large frying pan with a little low-calorie cooking oil spray and place over a high heat until hot. Add the chicken and cook for 4–5 minutes, turning until browned all over. Transfer to the slow cooker pot, packing them in tightly together.

Add the chopped onion mixture to the frying pan and cook for 2 minutes until just softened. Stir in the cinnamon, cumin, turmeric and peppercorns, then add the lemon juice and stock. Season to taste and bring to the boil, stirring.

Pour the hot stock over the chicken, cover and cook on Low for 7–8 hours until the chicken is cooked through and beginning to shrink on the bones. Stir the sauce, add the spinach, cover again and cook on High for 15–30 minutes until the spinach has wilted. Spoon into shallow bowls and serve immediately.

For Indian chicken & chickpea curry, follow the recipe above, using just 4 chicken drumsticks and adding ¼ teaspoon chilli powder instead of the black pepper. Place the browned drumsticks in the slow cooker pot with a 400 g (13 oz) can of chickpeas, drained, then pour over the hot stock and cook as above. **Calories per serving 123**

slow-cooked ratatouille

Calories per serving **135**
Serves **4**
Preparation time **20 minutes**
Cooking time **3¾–5 hours**

low-calorie cooking oil spray
1 **onion**, chopped
1 large **aubergine**, halved
  lengthways and sliced
2 **garlic cloves**, finely chopped
1 **red pepper**, cored,
  deseeded and diced
1 **orange pepper**, cored,
  deseeded and diced
400 g (13 oz) can **chopped**
  tomatoes
150 ml (¼ pint) **vegetable**
  stock
1 teaspoon **granular**
  sweetener
1 teaspoon **dried**
  Mediterranean herbs
2 teaspoons **cornflour**
500 g (1 lb) **courgettes**,
  thickly sliced
200 g (7 oz) **cherry tomatoes**,
  halved
salt and **pepper**
small handful of **basil leaves**,
  to garnish

Preheat the slow cooker if necessary. Spray a large frying pan with a little low-calorie cooking oil spray and place over a high heat until hot. Add the onion and aubergine and cook for 5 minutes until just beginning to brown.

Stir in the garlic, peppers, tomatoes, stock, sweetener and dried herbs, season to taste, then bring to the boil, stirring. Transfer to the slow cooker pot, cover and cook on High for 3–4 hours until the vegetables are tender.

Mix the cornflour to a smooth paste with a little cold water and stir into the pot with the courgettes and cherry tomatoes. Cover again and cook for 30–45 minutes until the courgettes are just tender. Garnish with basil and serve.

For ribollita, the Italian version of ratatouille, follow the recipe above, omitting the aubergine and adding a 400 g (13 oz) can of haricot beans, drained, to the frying pan with the stock. Cook as above, then stir in 125 g (4 oz) spinach leaves for the final 15 minutes of cooking. **Calories per serving 194**

thai broth with fish dumplings

Calories per serving **189**
Serves **4**
Preparation time **30 minutes**
Cooking time **2¼–3¼ hours**

900 ml (1½ pints) boiling **fish stock**
2 teaspoons **Thai fish sauce (nam pla)**
1 tablespoon **Thai red curry paste**
1 tablespoon **soy sauce**
½ bunch of **spring onions**, sliced
1 **carrot**, thinly sliced
2 **garlic cloves**, finely chopped
1 bunch of **asparagus**, trimmed and stems cut into 4
2 **pak choi**, thickly sliced

Dumplings
½ bunch of **spring onions**, sliced
15 g (½ oz) **coriander leaves**
3.5 cm (1½ inches) **fresh root ginger**, peeled and sliced
400 g (13 oz) **cod**, skinned
1 tablespoon **cornflour**
1 **egg white**

Preheat the slow cooker if necessary. Make the dumplings. Put half of the spring onions into a food processor with the coriander and ginger and chop finely. Add the cod, cornflour and egg white and process until the fish is finely chopped. With wetted hands, shape the mixture into 12 balls.

Pour the boiling fish stock into the slow cooker pot, add the fish sauce, curry paste and soy sauce. Add the spring onions, the carrot and garlic and drop in the dumplings. Cover with the lid and cook on Low for 2–3 hours.

When almost ready to serve, add the asparagus and pak choi to the broth. Replace the lid and cook on High for 15 minutes or until just tender. Ladle into bowls and serve.

For Thai broth with noodles & prawns, prepare and cook the broth as above, omitting the dumplings, for 2–3 hours. Add the asparagus, pak choi and 200 g (7 oz) frozen large prawns, thoroughly thawed, and cook for 15 minutes on High. Meanwhile, soak 75 g (3 oz) rice noodles in boiling water according to the packet instructions. Drain and add to the bottom of 4 soup bowls. Ladle the broth on top and sprinkle with a little chopped coriander. **Calories per serving 185**

spinach & courgette tian

Calories per serving **180**
Serves **4**
Preparation time **20 minutes**
Cooking time **1¾–2¼ hours**

50 g (2 oz) **long-grain rice**
1 tablespoon **olive oil**, plus
  extra for greasing
1 **tomato**, sliced
½ **onion**, chopped
1 **garlic clove**, finely chopped
175 g (6 oz) **courgettes**,
  coarsely grated
125 g (4 oz) **spinach**, thickly
  shredded
3 **eggs**
6 tablespoons **milk**
pinch of grated **nutmeg**
4 tablespoons chopped **mint**
salt and **pepper**

Preheat the slow cooker if necessary. Cook the rice in a saucepan of lightly salted boiling water according to packet instructions until tender.

Meanwhile, grease the base and sides of a 14 cm (5½ inch) round ovenproof dish, about 9 cm (3½ inches) deep, with a little oil and line the base with nonstick baking paper. Arrange the tomato slices, overlapping, in the bottom of the dish.

Heat the oil in a frying pan over a medium heat, add the onion and cook for 5 minutes until softened. Stir in the garlic, courgette and spinach and cook for 2 minutes or until the spinach has just wilted.

Beat together the eggs, milk and nutmeg and season to taste. Drain the rice and stir into the spinach mixture with the egg mixture and mint. Mix well, then spoon into the dish. Cover loosely with greased foil and place in the slow cooker pot.

Pour boiling water into the slow cooker pot to come halfway up the sides of the dish, cover and cook on High for 1½–2 hours or until the tian is set in the middle. Remove from the slow cooker, leave to stand for 5 minutes, then remove the foil, loosen the edges and turn out on to a plate. Cut into wedges and serve warm with salad, if liked.

For cheesy spinach & pine nut tian, follow the recipe above, omitting the courgette and stirring 50 g (2 oz) freshly grated Parmesan cheese, a small bunch of chopped basil and 4 tablespoons toasted pine nuts into the mixture instead of the mint.
Calories per serving 299

chicken noodle broth

Calories per serving **133**
Serves **4**
Preparation time **10 minutes**
Cooking time **5 hours 20 minutes–7½ hours**

1 **chicken carcass**
1 **onion**, cut into wedges
2 **carrots**, sliced
2 **celery sticks**, sliced
1 **bouquet garni**
1.2 litres (2 pints) **boiling water**
75 g (3 oz) **vermicelli pasta**
4 tablespoons chopped **parsley**
salt and **pepper**

Preheat the slow cooker if necessary. Place the chicken carcass in the slow cooker pot, breaking it into 2 pieces if necessary to make it fit. Add the onion, carrots, celery and bouquet garni. Pour over the boiling water and season to taste. Cover and cook on High for 5–7 hours.

Strain the soup through a large sieve, then return the liquid to the slow cooker pot. Remove any meat from the carcass and add to the pot. Adjust the seasoning if necessary, add the pasta and cook for a further 20–30 minutes until the pasta is just cooked. Sprinkle with the parsley, ladle into deep bowls and serve.

For chicken & minted pea soup, follow the recipe above to make the soup, then strain and pour it back into the slow cooker pot. Add 200 g (7 oz) finely sliced leeks, 375 g (12 oz) frozen peas and a small bunch of mint, cover and cook for a further 30 minutes. Purée the soup in a liquidizer or with a hand-held stick blender, then stir in 150 g (5 oz) mascarpone cheese until melted. Ladle into bowls and sprinkle with extra mint, if liked. **Calories per serving 255**

roasted vegetable terrine

Calories per serving **199**
Serves **4**
Preparation time **20 minutes,
  plus cooling**
Cooking time **2¼–3¼ hours**

375 g (12 oz) **courgettes**,
  thinly sliced
1 **red pepper**, cored,
  deseeded and quartered
1 **orange pepper**, cored,
  deseeded and quartered
2 tablespoons **olive oil**, plus
  extra for greasing
1 **garlic clove**, finely chopped
2 **eggs**
150 ml (¼ pint) **milk**
25 g (1 oz) **Parmesan
  cheese**, grated
3 tablespoons chopped **basil**
salt and **pepper**

Preheat the slow cooker if necessary. Line a grill rack with foil and arrange all the vegetables on it in a single layer, with the peppers skin sides up. Drizzle with the oil, sprinkle with the garlic and season with salt and pepper. Grill for 10 minutes or until softened and golden. Transfer the courgette slices to a plate and wrap the peppers in the foil. Leave to stand for 5 minutes to loosen the skins.

Oil a 500 g (1 lb) loaf tin and line the base and two long sides with nonstick baking paper, checking first it will fit in the slow cooker pot. Beat together the eggs, milk, Parmesan and basil in a bowl and season to taste. Unwrap the peppers and peel away the skins.

Arrange one-third of the courgette slices over the base and sides of the tin. Spoon in a little custard, then add half the peppers in a single layer and a little more custard. Repeat, ending with a layer of courgettes and custard. Cover the top with foil and put in the slow cooker pot.

Pour boiling water into the pot to come halfway up the sides of the tin, cover and cook on High for 2–3 hours or until the custard has set. Remove the tin from the slow cooker and leave to cool.

Loosen the edges of the terrine with a round-bladed knife, turn out on to a plate and peel off the lining paper. Cut into slices and serve with romesco sauce, if liked.

For romesco sauce, to serve as an accompaniment, cook 1 chopped onion in 1 tablespoon olive oil in a frying pan for 5 minutes until softened. Add 2 chopped garlic cloves, 4 skinned and chopped tomatoes, ½ teaspoon paprika and 40 g (1½ oz) finely chopped almonds. Simmer for 10 minutes until thick, season to taste and allow to cool. **Calories per serving 125**

baked honey & orange custards

Calories per serving **144**
Serves **4**
Preparation time **15 minutes,
   plus cooling and chilling**
Cooking time **4–5 hours**

2 **eggs**
2 **egg yolks**
400 ml (14 fl oz) **semi-
   skimmed milk**
3 teaspoons **granular
   sweetener**
3 teaspoons **runny honey**
½ teaspoon **vanilla extract**
finely grated rind of ½ **orange,
   plus extra to garnish**
large pinch of **ground
   cinnamon**

Preheat the slow cooker if necessary. Place the eggs, egg yolks and milk in a mixing bowl with the sweetener, honey and vanilla and whisk together until smooth. Strain the mixture through a sieve into a large jug, then whisk in the orange rind.

Divide the mixture between 4 x 150 ml (¼ pint) ovenproof dishes (checking first that the dishes fit in your slow cooker pot). Place the dishes in the slow cooker pot and sprinkle the cinnamon over the top. Pour hot water into the slow cooker pot until it comes halfway up the sides of the dishes. Cover the tops of the dishes with foil, place the lid on the slow cooker and cook on Low for 4–5 hours until set.

Remove the dishes from the slow cooker and leave to cool. Transfer to the refrigerator to chill well before serving, garnished with a little extra orange rind.

For vanilla crème brulée, follow the recipe above to cook and chill the custards, using 1 teaspoon vanilla extract and omitting the orange rind and cinnamon. Just before serving, sprinkle 1 teaspoon caster sugar over the top of each dish and caramelize the sugar with a cook's blow torch or under a preheated hot grill. Cool for a few minutes to allow the sugar to set hard, then serve with a few fresh raspberries. **Calories per serving 193**

baked apples with blackberries

Calories per serving **95**
Serves **4**
Preparation time **15 minutes**
Cooking time **3–3½ hours**

4 **Gala dessert apples**, 425 g
  (14 oz) in total
150 g (5 oz) **blackberries**
1 tablespoon **blackberry** or
  blueberry jam
6 tablespoons **pressed apple**
  juice

Preheat the slow cooker if necessary. Use an apple corer or small knife to remove the cores from the apples, then enlarge the holes slightly at the top and place the apples in the slow cooker pot.

Press a few of the blackberries into the apple cavities, then dot with jam. Push the remaining berries into the cavities, then pour the apple juice into the slow cooker pot. Cover and cook on High for 3–3½ hours until the apples are soft but still a bright colour.

Serve in shallow bowls with some of the juice spooned over.

For Christmas baked apples, core the apples as above and place in the slow cooker pot. Mix 4 teaspoons Christmas mincemeat with a large pinch of ground cinnamon and 40 g (1½ oz) diced ready-to-eat dried apricots. Use the mixture to fill the apples, pour 6 tablespoons apple juice into the slow cooker pot and cook as above. **Calories per serving 119**

apricot & cardamom fool

Calories per serving **126**
Serves **4**
Preparation time **15 minutes,
 plus cooling and chilling**
Cooking time **1½–2 hours**

325 g (11 oz) **apricots,**
 halved, stoned and cut into
 chunks
2 **cardamom pods,** crushed
1 tablespoon **runny honey**
4 tablespoons **water**
150 g (5 oz) **ready-made
 custard**
150 g (5 oz) **fromage frais**

Preheat the slow cooker if necessary. Place the apricots in the slow cooker pot with the crushed cardamom pods and their black seeds. Drizzle over the honey and water, cover and cook on Low for 1½–2 hours until the apricots are soft.

Remove the pot from the slow cooker and leave to cool for 30 minutes. Discard the cardamom pods and purée the fruit in a liquidizer or with a hand-held stick blender.

Mix the custard with the fromage frais and place a spoonful in each of 4 serving glasses. Add a spoonful of the fruit mixture and continue alternating custard and fruit to fill the glasses. Swirl the ingredients together with the handle of a teaspoon and chill until ready to serve.

For plum & cinnamon fool, place 325 g (11 oz) chopped ripe red plums in the slow cooker pot with ½ teaspoon ground cinnamon, 1 tablespoon runny honey and 4 tablespoons water. Cook as above, allow to cool, then purée. Swirl with the custard and fromage frais, chill and serve as for the main recipe. **Calories per serving 131**

baked peaches with ginger

Calories per serving **105**
Serves **4**
Preparation time **10 minutes**
Cooking time **1½–2½ hours**

2.5 cm (1 inch) piece of **fresh
  root ginger**, finely chopped
6 ripe **peaches**, halved and
  stoned
6 tablespoons **pressed apple
  juice**
1 tablespoon **caster sugar**
75 g (3 oz) **blueberries**
150 ml (¼ pint) **0% fat Greek
  yogurt**

Preheat the slow cooker if necessary. Arrange the
chopped ginger over the base of the slow cooker pot,
then place the peaches, cut sides down, on top in a
single layer. Pour over the apple juice, then sprinkle
with the sugar and blueberries.

Cover and cook on Low for 1½–2½ hours until the
peaches are piping hot and the juices are beginning
to run from the blueberries. Spoon into serving bowls
and serve warm or cold with the Greek yogurt.

For baked peaches with rosé wine, arrange
8 peach halves, cut sides down, in the base of the
slow cooker pot and pour over 6 tablespoons rosé
wine, 1 tablespoon caster sugar and 125 g (4 oz)
raspberries instead of the blueberries. Cover, cook
and serve as above. **Calories per serving 100**

plum & blueberry swirl

Calories per serving **110**
Serves **4**
Preparation time **15 minutes**
Cooking time **2¼–2¾ hours**

300 g (10 oz) ripe **red plums**,
 halved, stoned and cut into
 chunks
150 g (5 oz) **blueberries**
1 tablespoon **granular**
 sweetener
juice of ½ **orange**
3 tablespoons **water**
1 tablespoon **cornflour**

Yogurt
200 g (7 oz) **0% fat Greek**
 yogurt
finely grated rind of ½ **orange**
1 tablespoon **granular**
 sweetener

Preheat the slow cooker if necessary. Place the plums and blueberries in the slow cooker pot, sprinkle with the sweetener, then add the orange juice and water. Cover and cook on High for 2–2½ hours until the fruit is soft.

Mix the cornflour to a smooth paste with a little cold water and stir into the pot. Cover again and cook for a further 15 minutes until thickened, stir the fruit and leave to cool.

Mix the yogurt with the orange rind and sweetener. Divide the fruit between 4 serving glasses, top with the yogurt, then swirl together with a teaspoon. Chill until ready to serve.

For minted strawberry & blueberry swirl, place 300 g (10 oz) ripe strawberries in the slow cooker pot with 150 g (5 oz) blueberries, 1 tablespoon sweetener and the juice of ½ orange. Cook as above, then thicken with the cornflour, cook for a further 15 minutes and leave to cool. Mix 200 g (7 oz) 0% fat Greek yogurt with 1 tablespoon chopped mint and 1 tablespoon granular sweetener, then swirl with the fruit as above.
Calories per serving 102

spiced pears

Calories per serving **83**
Serves **4**
Preparation time **15 minutes**
Cooking time **3–4 hours**

300 ml (½ pint) **hot water**
4 **cardamom pods**, crushed
7.5 cm (3 inch) **cinnamon stick**, halved
2.5 cm (1 inch) piece of **fresh root ginger**, thinly sliced
2 teaspoons **granular sweetener**
4 **pears** with stalks, peeled, halved lengthways and cored
pared rind and juice of
   1 **lemon**
pared rind and juice of
   1 **orange**

Preheat the slow cooker if necessary. Pour the hot water into the slow cooker pot, then stir in the cardamom pods and their black seeds, the cinnamon, ginger and sweetener.

Add the pears and the lemon and orange juice, then gently turn the pears in the liquid to coat and arrange them cut sides down in a single layer. Cut the pared lemon and orange rind into very thin strips and sprinkle on top.

Cover and cook on Low for 3–4 hours until the pears are tender. The cooking time will depend on their ripeness. Serve warm.

For mulled wine pears, follow the recipe above, using 150 ml (¼ pint) red wine and 150 ml (¼ pint) hot water instead of 300 ml (½ pint) hot water, and using 4 cloves instead of the cardamom pods. Increase the sweetener to 3 teaspoons, or to taste, and cook as above. **Calories per serving 99**

recipes under 300 calories

vanilla breakfast prunes & figs

Calories per serving **299**
Serves **4**
Preparation time **5 minutes**
Cooking time **8—10 hours** or
  overnight

1 **breakfast tea** teabag
600 ml (1 pint) boiling **water**
150 g (5 oz) pitted **prunes**
150 g (5 oz) dried **figs**
75 g (3 oz) **caster sugar**
1 teaspoon **vanilla extract**
pared rind of ½ **orange**

To serve
natural **yogurt**
muesli

Preheat the slow cooker if necessary. Put the teabag into a jug or teapot, add the boiling water and leave to soak for 2—3 minutes. Remove the teabag and pour the tea into the slow cooker pot.

Add the whole prunes and figs, the sugar and vanilla extract to the hot tea, sprinkle with the orange rind and mix together. Cover with the lid and cook on low for 8—10 hours or overnight.

Serve hot with spoonfuls of natural yogurt and a sprinkling of muesli.

For breakfast apricots in orange, put 300 g (10 oz) dried apricots, 50 g (2 oz) caster sugar, 300 ml (½ pint) boiling water and 150 ml (¼ pint) orange juice in the slow cooker pot. Cover and cook as above. **Calories per serving 295**

brunch poached eggs & haddock

Calories per serving **247**
Serves **2**
Preparation time **5 minutes**
Cooking time **1–1¼ hours**

low-calorie cooking oil spray
2 **eggs**
1 teaspoon chopped **chives**
2 **smoked haddock steaks**,
    125 g (4 oz) each
450 ml (¾ pint) boiling **water**
125 g (4 oz) **baby spinach**
10 g (½ oz) **butter**
salt and **pepper**

Preheat the slow cooker if necessary. Spray the insides of 2 small ovenproof dishes or ramekins with a little low-calorie cooking oil spray, then break an egg into each. Sprinkle with a few chives and season to taste.

Place the egg dishes in the centre of the slow cooker pot, then arrange a fish steak on each side. Pour the boiling water over the fish so that the water comes halfway up the sides of the dishes. Cover and cook on High for 1–1¼ hours until the eggs are done to your liking and the fish flakes easily when pressed with a small knife.

Rinse the spinach with a little water, drain and place in a microwave-proof dish. Cover and cook in a microwave on full power for 1 minute until just wilted. Divide between 2 serving plates, and top with the fish steaks. Loosen the eggs with a knife and turn out of their dishes on top of the fish. Sprinkle with chopped chives, season with salt and pepper and serve.

For brunch poached eggs with salmon, follow the recipe above, using 2 wild salmon steaks, 100 g (3½ oz) each, instead of the smoked haddock. Arrange 2 sliced tomatoes on the serving plates, top with the cooked salmon and eggs and serve. **Calories per serving 291**

baked eggs with toast

Calories per serving **295**
Serves **4**
Preparation time **15 minutes**
Cooking time **40–50 minutes**

25 g (1 oz) **butter**
4 thin slices of **honey roast ham**, 65 g (2½ oz) in total
4 teaspoons **spicy tomato chutney**
4 **eggs**
2 **cherry tomatoes**, halved
1 **spring onion**, finely sliced
salt and **pepper**
4 slices of thinly spread buttered **toast**, to serve

Preheat the slow cooker if necessary. Use a little of the butter to grease 4 x 150 ml (¼ pint) ovenproof dishes (checking first that the dishes fit in your slow cooker pot). Press a slice of ham into each dish to line the base and sides, leaving a small overhang of ham above the dish.

Place 1 teaspoon of chutney in the base of each dish, then break an egg on top. Add a cherry tomato half to each, sprinkle with the spring onion, season to taste, then dot with the remaining butter. Cover the tops with greased foil and put in the slow cooker pot.

Pour boiling water into the slow cooker pot to come halfway up the sides of the dishes, cover and cook on High for 40–50 minutes or until the egg whites are set and the yolks still slightly soft.

Remove the foil and gently run a round-bladed knife between the ham and the edges of the dishes. Turn out and quickly turn the baked eggs the right way up. Place each on a plate and serve with the hot buttered toast, cut into fingers.

For eggs Benedict, butter 4 dishes as above, then break an egg into each. Season to taste, sprinkle the eggs with 1 sliced spring onion and dot with 25 g (1 oz) butter. Cover and cook as above. To serve, grill 8 back bacon rashers until golden. Toast 4 halved English breakfast muffins, spread with butter, divide the bacon between the lower halves and arrange on serving plates. Top with the baked eggs and drizzle with 4 tablespoons warmed ready-made hollandaise sauce. Replace the muffin tops and serve immediately. **Calories per serving 492**

hearty winter sausage stew

Calories per serving **299**
Serves **4**
Preparation time **20 minutes**
Cooking time **5¼–6¼ hours**

low-calorie cooking oil spray
50 g (2 oz) **smoked back
    bacon**, trimmed of fat and
    chopped
1 **red onion**, chopped
½ teaspoon **smoked hot
    paprika** or **chilli powder**
300 ml (½ pint) **chicken stock**
400 g (13 oz) can **reduced-
    sugar baked beans**
450 g (14½ oz) **extra-lean
    sausages**
1 **red pepper**, cored,
    deseeded and chopped
400 g (13 oz) peeled
    pumpkin, diced
2 **celery sticks**, thickly sliced
2 **sage sprigs** or ½ teaspoon
    dried sage
salt and **pepper**

Preheat the slow cooker if necessary. Spray a large frying pan with a little low-calorie cooking oil spray and place over a high heat until hot. Add the bacon and onion and fry for 4–5 minutes, stirring until just beginning to brown. Stir in the paprika, then pour in the stock and baked beans. Season to taste, then bring to the boil, stirring.

Arrange the sausages in a single layer in the base of the slow cooker pot, top with the red pepper, pumpkin, celery and sage, then pour over the hot stock and beans. Cover and cook on High for 5–6 hours. Stir the stew, spoon into shallow bowls and serve.

For bonfire night chicken stew, follow the recipe above, using 625 g (1 ¼ lb) boneless, skinless chicken thighs instead of the sausages, and browning it with the bacon and onion. Add to the slow cooker pot with the vegetables, pour over the hot stock and beans, cover and cook on Low for 7–8 hours. **Calories per serving 315**

braised trout with warm puy lentils

Calories per serving **279**
Serves **4**
Preparation time **20 minutes**
Cooking time **2½–3 hours**

400 g (13 oz) can **Puy lentils**,
  drained
2 tablespoons **balsamic
  vinegar**
4 **spring onions**, chopped
3 **tomatoes**, chopped
4 thick **trout steaks**, 150 g
  (5 oz) each
finely grated rind and juice of
  ½ **lemon**
leaves from 2–3 **thyme sprigs**
large pinch of **dried chilli
  flakes**
150 ml (¼ pint) hot **fish stock**
salt and **pepper**
50 g (2 oz) **rocket leaves**, to
  serve

Preheat the slow cooker if necessary. Place the lentils in the slow cooker pot, then stir in the balsamic vinegar, spring onions and tomatoes.

Arrange the trout steaks on top in a single layer, then sprinkle with the lemon rind and juice, thyme leaves and chilli flakes and season to taste. Pour the stock around the trout steaks, then cover and cook on Low for 2½–3 hours or until the trout is cooked through and flakes easily when pressed with a small knife.

Divide the rocket leaves between 4 serving plates. Arrange the trout and lentils on top and spoon over a little of the stock. Serve immediately.

For smoked cod & spinach salad, follow the recipe above, using 100 g (3½ oz) sliced button mushrooms instead of the tomatoes, and 4 thick smoked cod loin steaks, 150 g (5 oz) each, instead of the trout. After cooking, stir 50 g (2 oz) baby spinach leaves into the lentil mixture and serve each portion topped with a poached egg. **Calories per serving 228**

turkey with cranberries & pumpkin

Calories per serving **270**
**(not including steamed
  greens and broccoli)**
Serves **4**
Preparation time **20 minutes**
Cooking time **6¼–8¼ hours**

low-calorie cooking oil spray
500 g (1 lb) **turkey breast,**
  diced
1 **onion**, chopped
2 teaspoons **plain flour**
300 ml (½ pint) **chicken stock**
juice of 1 large **orange**
½ teaspoon **ground mixed
  spice**
30 g (1¼ oz) **dried
  cranberries**
500 g (1 lb) peeled **pumpkin,**
  cut into 2.5 cm (1 inch)
  cubes
salt and **pepper**

Preheat the slow cooker if necessary. Spray a large frying pan with a little low-calorie cooking oil spray and place over a high heat until hot. Add the turkey, a few pieces at a time until all the turkey is in the pan. Add the onion and cook for 5 minutes, stirring and turning the turkey pieces until golden.

Sprinkle in the flour and stir well. Add the stock, orange juice, mixed spice and cranberries and season to taste. Bring to the boil, stirring.

Place the pumpkin in the slow cooker pot and pour the turkey mixture on top, pushing the turkey pieces into the liquid. Cover and cook on Low for 6–8 hours until the turkey is cooked through. Spoon into shallow dishes and serve with steamed green beans and broccoli, if liked.

For turkey curry with sultanas & pumpkin, follow the recipe above but omit the mixed spice and cranberries and add 3 teaspoons medium-hot curry powder and 25 g (1 oz) sultanas instead. **Calories per serving 279**

chunky chicken & basil stew

Calories per serving **262**
Serves **4**
Preparation time **20 minutes**
Cooking time **8½–10¾ hours**

low-calorie cooking oil spray
625 g (1¼ lb) boneless,
    skinless **chicken thighs**,
    each cut into 3 pieces
1 **onion**, chopped
2 small **carrots**, finely diced
2 teaspoons **plain flour**
350 ml (12 fl oz) **chicken
    stock**
15 g (½ oz) **basil leaves**, torn,
    plus extra to garnish
100 g (3½ oz) **frozen peas**,
    defrosted
200 g (7 oz) **Tenderstem
    broccoli**, stems cut into 3 or
    4 pieces
150 g (5 oz) **fine green
    beans**, thickly sliced
salt and **pepper**

Preheat the slow cooker if necessary. Spray a large frying pan with a little low-calorie cooking oil spray and place over a high heat until hot. Add the chicken, a few pieces at a time until all the chicken is in the pan, and cook for 5 minutes, stirring, until golden. Transfer to the slow cooker pot using a slotted spoon.

Add a little more low-calorie cooking oil spray to the pan if necessary, then cook the onion for 4–5 minutes until just beginning to soften. Stir in the carrots and flour, then add the stock and bring to the boil, stirring. Add the basil, season to taste and pour over the chicken. Cover and cook on Low for 8–10 hours until the chicken is tender and cooked through.

Add the peas, broccoli and green beans, cover again and cook on High for 15–30 minutes until the vegetables are tender. Serve in shallow bowls, garnished with extra basil.

For chunky chicken with 30 garlic cloves, brown 625 g (1¼ lb) boneless, skinless chicken thighs, each cut into 3 pieces, in a frying pan and place in the slow cooker pot with 30 unpeeled garlic cloves. Follow the recipe above, using 250 g (8 oz) small peeled shallots instead of the onion and carrot, and 3 thyme sprigs and 2 teaspoons Dijon mustard instead of the basil. Cook as above, omitting the green vegetables, and serve sprinkled with chopped parsley. **Calories per serving 225**

caribbean brown stew trout

Calories per serving **293**
Serves **4**
Preparation time **20 minutes**
Cooking time **1½—2 hours**

4 small **trout**, gutted, heads
  and fins removed and well
  rinsed with cold water
1 teaspoon **ground allspice**
1 teaspoon **paprika**
1 teaspoon **ground coriander**
2 tablespoons **olive oil**
6 **spring onions**, thickly sliced
1 **red pepper**, cored,
  deseeded and thinly sliced
2 **tomatoes**, roughly chopped
½ **red hot bonnet** or other
  red chilli, deseeded and
  chopped
2 sprigs of **thyme**
300 ml (½ pint) **fish stock**
salt and **pepper**

Preheat the slow cooker if necessary. Slash the trout on each side 2—3 times with a sharp knife. Mix the spices and a little salt and pepper on a plate, then dip each side of the trout in the spice mix.

Heat the oil in a frying pan, add the trout and fry until browned on both sides but not cooked all the way through. Drain and arrange in the slow cooker pot so that they fit snugly in a single layer.

Add the remaining ingredients to the frying pan with any spices left on the plate and bring to the boil, stirring. Pour over the trout, then cover with the lid and cook on High for 1½—2 hours or until the fish breaks into flakes when pressed in the centre with a knife.

Lift the fish carefully out of the slow cooker pot using a fish slice and transfer to shallow dishes. Spoon the sauce over and serve.

For brown stew chicken, use 8 chicken thigh joints instead of the trout. Slash and dip in the spice mix as above. Fry in the olive oil until browned, then drain and transfer to the slow cooker pot. Heat the vegetables as above using 450 ml (¾ pint) chicken stock instead of fish stock, season, then cook with the chicken joints in the slow cooker on Low for 8—10 hours. Thicken the sauce if liked with 4 teaspoons cornflour mixed with a little water, stir into the sauce and cook for 15 minutes more. **Calories per serving 331**

coconut, pumpkin & chickpea curry

Calories per serving **236**
Serves **4**
Preparation time **25 minutes**
Cooking time **6¼–8¼ hours**

2 **onions**
2 **garlic cloves**, halved
4 cm (1½ inch) piece of **fresh
root ginger**, sliced
1 **red chilli**, quartered and
deseeded
low-calorie cooking oil spray
1½ tablespoons **medium
curry powder**
1 teaspoon **fennel seeds**,
roughly crushed
200 ml (7 fl oz) **full-fat
coconut milk**
300 ml (½ pint) **vegetable
stock**
2 teaspoons **granular
sweetener**
650 g (1 lb 5 oz) peeled
pumpkin, cut into 4 cm
(1½ inch) chunks
400 g (13 oz) can **chickpeas**,
drained
1 teaspoon **black mustard seeds**
15 g (½ oz) **fresh coriander**,
roughly torn
juice of 1 **lime**
salt and **pepper**

Preheat the slow cooker if necessary. Quarter 1 of the onions and place with the onion, garlic, ginger and chilli in a food processor and blitz until very finely chopped. Alternatively, chop the ingredients finely with a knife. Spray a large frying pan with a little low-calorie cooking oil spray and place over a high heat until hot. Add the onion paste and cook for 2 minutes, then stir in the curry powder and fennel seeds.

Add the coconut milk, stock and sweetener, then season to taste. Bring to the boil, stirring. Place the pumpkin and chickpeas in the slow cooker pot and pour the coconut mixture on top. Cover and cook on Low for 6–8 hours until the pumpkin is tender.

Make a crispy onion topping by slicing the remaining onion. Heat a little low-calorie cooking oil spray in a clean frying pan and cook the onion over a medium heat for 5 minutes until softened. Stir in the mustard seeds and cook for a few minutes more until the onion is golden and crispy. Stir the coriander and lime juice into the curry, spoon into bowls and served topped with the crispy onions.

**For creamy coconut, aubergine & chickpea
curry**, follow the recipe above, using 625 g (1¼ lb) aubergines, trimmed and diced, instead of the pumpkin.
Calories per serving 246

tandoori chicken

Calories per serving **208**
Serves **4**
Preparation time **20 minutes,
    plus marinating**
Cooking time **3¼–4¼ hours**

150 ml (¼ pint) **0% fat Greek
    yogurt**
4 cm (1½ inch) piece of **fresh
    root ginger**, grated
3 tablespoons chopped **fresh
    coriander leaves**
3 teaspoons **medium-hot
    curry powder**
½ teaspoon **ground turmeric**
1 teaspoon **paprika**
625 g (1¼ lb) boneless,
    skinless **chicken thighs**, cut
    into chunks
juice of ½ **lemon**
low-calorie cooking oil spray
salt and **pepper**

To serve
50 g (2 oz) **mixed green
    salad leaves**
¼ **cucumber**, diced
small handful of **fresh
    coriander leaves**
juice of ½ **lemon**

Place the yogurt in a mixing bowl and stir in the ginger, coriander, curry powder, turmeric and paprika. Toss the chicken with the lemon juice, season lightly and stir into the yogurt mixture until evenly coated. Cover the bowl and chill overnight.

Preheat the slow cooker if necessary. Stir the chicken mixture, then transfer to the slow cooker pot in an even layer. Cover and cook on High for 3–4 hours or until the chicken is tender and cooked through. (The yogurt will separate during cooking but this will not affect the taste.)

Spray a large frying pan with a little low-calorie cooking oil spray and place over a high heat until hot. Transfer the chicken to the frying pan, a few pieces at a time until all the chicken is in the pan, and cook for 2–3 minutes, turning once, until golden on both sides. This step can be omitted if you are short of time.

Toss the salad leaves, cucumber and coriander leaves with the lemon juice, arrange on serving plates and top with the chicken.

For garlicky tandoori chicken, add 3 finely chopped garlic cloves to the yogurt and spice mixture and continue as above. **Calories per serving 209**

chilli, mushroom & tomato ragu

Calories per serving **295**
Serves **4**
Preparation time **20 minutes**
Cooking time **7¼–8¼ hours**

1 tablespoon **olive oil**
1 **red onion**, roughly chopped
2 **garlic cloves**, finely chopped
1 teaspoon **paprika**
½ teaspoon **dried chilli flakes**
1 teaspoon **dried Mediterranean herbs**
400 g (13 oz) **passata**
2 teaspoons **granular sweetener**
300 g (10 oz) small **button mushrooms**
300 g (10 oz) **cherry tomatoes**
salt and **pepper**

To serve
200 g (7 oz) **dried penne pasta**
large pinch of **dried chilli flakes** (optional)
handful of **rocket leaves**

Preheat the slow cooker if necessary. Heat the oil a large frying pan over a medium heat until hot, add the onion and cook for 4–5 minutes, stirring until just beginning to soften. Add the garlic, paprika and chilli flakes, then the dried herbs, passata and sweetener. Season to taste and bring to the boil.

Place the mushrooms and cherry tomatoes in the slow cooker pot, pour over the hot passata mixture and stir well. Cover and cook on Low for 7–8 hours.

Cook the pasta in a saucepan of lightly salted boiling water according to packet instructions until tender. Drain and stir into the ragu, then spoon into shallow bowls and sprinkle with a few extra dried chilli flakes, if liked, and top with the rocket. Serve immediately.

For courgette & tomato arrabiata, follow the recipe above, using 200 g (7 oz) diced courgette and 1 cored, deseeded and diced red pepper instead of the mushrooms. **Calories per serving 307**

74

corn & smoked cod chowder

Calories per serving **207**
Serves **4**
Preparation time **20 minutes**
Cooking time **2¼–3¼ hours**

low-calorie cooking oil spray
1 **leek**, thinly sliced
50 g (2 oz) **smoked back
 bacon**, trimmed of fat and
 diced
200 g (7 oz) **potato**, finely
 diced
175 g (6 oz) **celeriac**, finely
 diced
75 g (3 oz) **frozen sweetcorn
 kernels**
450 ml (¾ pint) **fish stock**
1 **bay leaf**
250 g (8 oz) **smoked cod
 fillet**
200 ml (7 fl oz) **skimmed milk**
50 g (2 oz) **reduced-fat
 cream cheese**
salt and **pepper**
chopped **parsley**, to garnish

Preheat the slow cooker if necessary. Spray a large
frying pan with a little low-calorie cooking oil spray and
place over a medium heat until hot. Add the white leek
slices (reserving the green slices) and the bacon and
cook for 3–4 minutes until the leeks have softened and
the bacon is just beginning to brown.

Add the potato, celeriac, sweetcorn and stock. Bring
to the boil, stirring, then add the bay leaf and season to
taste. Transfer to the slow cooker pot, arrange the fish
on top and press the fish into the liquid. Cover and cook
on High for 2–3 hours until the potatoes and celeriac
are tender and the fish flakes easily when pressed with
a small knife. Transfer the fish to a plate, remove the
skin and bones and break into pieces.

Stir the milk and cream cheese into the slow cooker
pot, then stir in the reserved green leek slices and
the flaked fish. Cover again and cook for 15 minutes
until the leeks are tender. Ladle into bowls and serve
garnished with the chopped parsley.

For salmon & crab chowder, follow the recipe above,
using 250 g (8 oz) salmon fillet instead of the smoked
cod. Cook as above, stirring in a 40 g (1½ oz) can of
dark crab meat for the last 15 minutes of cooking time.
Calories per serving 249

baba ganoush

Calories per serving **239**
Serves **4**
Preparation time **20 minutes**
Cooking time **3–4 hours**

1 large **aubergine**, 300 g
  (10 oz), halved lengthways
1 tablespoon **olive oil**
2 tablespoons **0% fat Greek
  yogurt**
3 tablespoons chopped **fresh
  coriander leaves**
1 large **garlic clove**, finely
  chopped
juice of ½ **lemon**
seeds from ¼ **pomegranate**
salt and **pepper**

To serve
4 **pitta breads**
1 **red pepper**, cored,
  deseeded and cut into
  batons
½ **cucumber**, deseeded and
  cut into batons

Preheat the slow cooker if necessary. Cut criss-cross lines over the cut side of each aubergine half, rub with salt and pepper, then drizzle with the oil. Arrange, cut sides down, in the base of the slow cooker pot, cover and cook on High for 3–4 hours or until the aubergines are soft. Leave to cool.

Use a spoon to scoop the flesh out of the aubergine skins and chop it roughly. Place in a mixing bowl with the yogurt, coriander leaves, garlic and lemon juice. Season to taste, spoon into a serving dish and scatter with the pomegranate seeds.

Warm the pitta breads under a preheated hot grill, then cut into thick strips. Arrange on a serving plate with the pepper and cucumber batons and serve with the baba ganoush.

For grilled steaks with aubergine sauce, make the baba ganoush following the recipe above. Trim the fat from 4 sirloin steaks, 125 g (4 oz) each, and season to taste. Spray with a little low-calorie cooking oil spray and cook on a preheated hot ridged griddle pan for 2–3 minutes, turning once, or until cooked to your liking. Serve the steaks with the baba ganoush and a rocket salad tossed with lemon juice. **Calories per serving 294**

tapenade-topped cod

Calories per serving **246**
Serves **4**
Preparation time **15 minutes**
Cooking time **3½–4 hours**

200 g (7 oz) **passata**
200 g (7 oz) **spinach**, rinsed
and drained
175 g (6 oz) **tomatoes**,
roughly chopped
50 g (2 oz) **chorizo**, diced
4 skinless **cod steaks**, 150 g
(5 oz) each
85 g (3¼ oz) **green olives
stuffed with hot pimento**
small handful of **basil leaves**,
plus extra to garnish
salt and **pepper**

Preheat the slow cooker if necessary. Spoon the passata over the base of the slow cooker pot, then arrange the spinach, tomatoes and chorizo in an even layer on top. Season to taste and place the fish steaks on top in a single layer, then season again.

Place the olives and basil in a food processor and blitz until finely chopped, or chop with a knife. Spread the mixture over the cod steaks, then cover and cook on Low for 3½ –4 hours until the fish is bright white and flakes easily when pressed with a small knife. Serve garnished with extra basil.

For herb-topped cod, mix 15 g (½ oz) finely chopped parsley and 15 g (½ oz) finely chopped basil with ½ teaspoon crushed cumin seeds and the grated rind of 1 lemon. Follow the recipe above, using this herb mixture to spread over the cod steaks before cooking instead of the olives and basil. **Calories per serving 249**

hot quinoa & pepper salad

Calories per serving **202**
Serves **4**
Preparation time **15 minutes**
Cooking time **3–4 hours**

3 **peppers**, cored, deseeded,
  and cut into chunks
2 **celery sticks**, sliced
2 **courgettes**, halved
  lengthways and thickly sliced
250 g (8 oz) **plum tomatoes**,
  roughly chopped
2 **garlic cloves**, finely chopped
125 g (4 oz) **quinoa and
  bulgar wheat grain mix**
4 tablespoons **red wine**
300 ml (½ pint) hot **vegetable
  stock**
1 tablespoon **tomato purée**
1 teaspoon **granular
  sweetener**
15 g (½ oz) **basil leaves**,
  roughly torn
salt and **pepper**

Preheat the slow cooker if necessary. Place the peppers, celery, courgettes and tomatoes in the slow cooker pot and sprinkle over the garlic and grain mix.

Mix the red wine with the stock, tomato purée and sweetener, season to taste and pour into the slow cooker pot. Stir the ingredients together, then cover and cook on High for 3–4 hours until the vegetables have softened and the grains have absorbed the liquid.

Stir the salad, then divide between 4 shallow bowls and serve topped with the torn basil leaves.

For hot quinoa & prawn salad, follow the recipe above to make the quinoa salad and divide between 4 bowls. Omit the basil and divide 100 g (3½ oz) mixed spinach, watercress and rocket leaves and 175 g (6 oz) cooked peeled prawns between the bowls. **Calories per serving 257**

asian turkey with rainbow chard

Calories per serving **234 (not including rice or noodles)**
Serves **4**
Preparation time **20 minutes**
Cooking time **8½–9¾ hours**

low-calorie cooking oil spray
500 g (1 lb) **turkey breast**, diced
1 **onion**, chopped
2 **garlic cloves**, finely chopped
200 g (7 oz) **closed-cap mushrooms**, sliced
450 ml (¾ pint) **chicken stock**
2.5 cm (1 inch) piece of **fresh root ginger**, chopped
2 tablespoons **soy sauce**
1 tablespoon **tamarind paste**
1 tablespoon **tomato purée**
1 tablespoon **cornflour**
200 g (7 oz) **rainbow chard**, thickly sliced

Preheat the slow cooker if necessary. Spray a large frying pan with a little low-calorie cooking oil spray and place over a high heat until hot. Add the turkey, a few pieces at a time until all the turkey is in the pan, and cook for 5 minutes, stirring, until golden. Transfer to the slow cooker pot using a slotted spoon.

Add a little extra low-calorie cooking oil spray to the frying pan, if necessary, and cook the onion for 4–5 minutes until softened. Stir in the garlic and mushrooms and cook for 2–3 minutes more. Add the stock, ginger, soy sauce, tamarind and tomato purée, season to taste and bring to the boil, stirring. Pour over the turkey, cover and cook on Low for 8–9 hours until the turkey is cooked through.

Mix the cornflour to a smooth paste with a little cold water and stir into the turkey mixture. Arrange the chard on top, cover again and cook on High for 15–30 minutes until tender. Spoon into bowls and serve with rice or noodles, if liked.

For black bean turkey, follow the recipe above to brown the turkey and fry the onion. Add the mushrooms to the frying pan with a 500 g (1 lb) jar of black bean cooking sauce and bring to the boil. Transfer to the slow cooker pot and cook as above. Stir-fry 275 g (9 oz) ready-prepared stir-fry vegetables in a little low-calorie cooking oil spray to serve with the turkey. **Calories per serving 294**

smoky sweet potato & quorn chilli

Calories per serving **299**
Serves **4**
Preparation time **20 minutes**
Cooking time **7¼–8¼ hours**

1–2 small **dried smoked chipotle chillies**
4 tablespoons boiling **water**
low-calorie cooking oil spray
1 **onion**, chopped
2 **garlic cloves**, finely chopped
1 teaspoon **ground cumin**
1 teaspoon **paprika**
2 x 400 g (13 oz) cans **chopped tomatoes**
400 g (13 oz) can **red kidney beans**, rinsed and drained
1 tablespoon **Worcestershire sauce** (optional)
350 g (11½ oz) **Quorn mince**
300 g (10 oz) **sweet potato**, cut into 2.5 cm (1 inch) cubes
salt and **pepper**

Salsa

½ **red onion**, finely chopped
3 tablespoons chopped **fresh coriander**
2 **tomatoes**, halved, deseeded and diced

Preheat the slow cooker if necessary. Place the dried chillies in a small bowl, pour over the boiling water and leave to stand for 10 minutes.

Spray a large frying pan with a little low-calorie cooking oil spray and place over a medium heat until hot. Add the onion, fry for 4–5 minutes until softened, then add the garlic, cumin and paprika. Stir in the tomatoes, kidney beans and Worcestershire sauce, if using, then the Quorn and sweet potato. Season to taste.

Finely chop the chillies, then stir into the Quorn mixture with the soaking water. Bring to the boil, stirring, then transfer to the slow cooker pot. Cover and cook on Low for 7–8 hours until the sweet potato is tender. Mix the salsa ingredients together, then sprinkle over the chilli to serve.

For sweet potato & soya mince curry, follow the recipe above, omitting the chipotle chillies. Add 1 teaspoon ground turmeric, 1 teaspoon garam masala and ½ teaspoon dried chilli flakes with the cumin and paprika, and a 400 g (13 oz) can lentils, drained, when adding the soya mince. Cook as above, then add 100 g (3½ oz) frozen peas and 4 tablespoons chopped fresh coriander, cover again and cook on High for 15 minutes. **Calories per serving 299**

aubergine parmigiana

Calories per serving **221**
Serves **4**
Preparation time **15 minutes**
Cooking time **4¼–5¼ hours**

1 tablespoon **olive oil**
1 **onion**, chopped
2 **garlic cloves**, finely chopped
400 g (13 oz) **tomatoes**,
    diced
400 g (13 oz) can **chopped
    tomatoes**
small handful of **basil**, torn,
    plus extra to garnish
2 teaspoons **granular
    sweetener**
2 teaspoons **cornflour**
2 large **aubergines**, sliced
75 g (3 oz) **mature Cheddar
    cheese**, grated
salt and **pepper**
2 tablespoons finely grated
    Parmesan cheese, to
    garnish

Preheat the slow cooker if necessary. Heat the oil in a large frying pan over a medium heat, add the onion and cook for 4–5 minutes until just beginning to soften. Add the garlic, fresh tomatoes, canned tomatoes, basil and sweetener. Mix the cornflour to a smooth paste with a little cold water and stir into the sauce. Season to taste and bring to the boil, stirring.

Spoon a little of the tomato sauce over the base of the slow cooker pot and arrange one-third of the aubergine slices, overlapping, on top. Spoon over a thin layer of the sauce and sprinkle with a little grated Cheddar. Repeat to make 3 aubergine layers, finishing with a generous layer of sauce and grated Cheddar.

Cover and cook on High for 4–5 hours until the aubergines are soft. Sprinkle with the Parmesan and extra basil and serve.

For mushroom parmigiana, follow the recipe above to make the tomato sauce, then layer in the slow cooker pot with 8 large flat field mushrooms, in 2 layers, and the Cheddar. Cook and serve as above. **Calories per serving 235**

easy cauliflower dahl

Calories per serving **211**
Serves **4**
Preparation time **15 minutes**
Cooking time **3–4 hours**

200 g (7 oz) **dried red lentils**,
  rinsed in cold water and
  drained
750 ml (1¼ pints) hot **water**
2 teaspoons **medium curry
  powder**
½ teaspoon **salt**
pepper

Spiced cauliflower
400 g (13 oz) **cauliflower**, cut
  into small florets
6 tablespoons **water**
1 **onion**, thinly sliced
low-calorie cooking oil spray
1 teaspoon **cumin seeds**,
  roughly crushed
1 teaspoon **ground turmeric**
1 teaspoon **garam masala**

Preheat the slow cooker if necessary. Place the lentils, hot water, curry powder and salt in the slow cooker pot, then season with pepper. Cover and cook on High for 3–4 hours or until the lentils are soft.

Meanwhile, place the cauliflower in a large frying pan with the water, cover and cook over a medium heat for 5 minutes until the cauliflower is almost tender. Drain off any excess water, then add the onion and a little low-calorie cooking oil spray, increase the heat and cook for 2–3 minutes, stirring.

Sprinkle the cumin, turmeric and garam masala over the cauliflower and cook, stirring, for 4–5 minutes until the cauliflower is golden brown. Season to taste. Stir the lentil dahl, spoon into shallow bowls and top with the spiced cauliflower.

For easy aubergine & mushroom dahl, follow the recipe above to cook the lentil dahl. Spray a large frying pan with a little low-calorie cooking oil spray, add 1 large diced aubergine and 100 g (3½ oz) sliced button mushrooms and cook over a medium heat for 2–3 minutes until beginning to soften. Add a little more low-calorie cooking oil spray, then the cumin, turmeric and garam masala as above and continue to cook until the aubergine is soft. Spoon over the dahl and sprinkle with chopped coriander. **Calories per serving 201**

lentil tagine with pomegranate

Calories per serving **276**
Serves **4**
Preparation time **15 minutes**
Cooking time **4–5 hours**

1 tablespoon **olive oil**
1 **onion**, chopped
5 cm (2 inch) piece of **fresh root ginger**, finely chopped
3 **garlic cloves**, finely chopped
2 teaspoons **cumin seeds**, crushed
1 teaspoon **coriander seeds**, crushed
200 g (7 oz) **dried Puy lentils**
2 **celery sticks**, sliced
250 g (8 oz) **cherry tomatoes**, halved
450 ml (¾ pint) hot **vegetable stock**
juice of 1 **lemon**
15 g (½ oz) **flat-leaf parsley**, roughly chopped
15 g (½ oz) **mint**, roughly chopped
salt and **pepper**

To serve
125 ml (4 fl oz) **0% fat Greek yogurt**
1 tablespoon **harissa**
seeds from ½ **pomegranate**

Preheat the slow cooker if necessary. Heat the oil in a large frying pan over a medium heat, add the onion and cook for 4–5 minutes until just beginning to soften. Stir in the ginger, garlic, cumin and coriander seeds.

Place the lentils in a sieve and rinse under cold running water. Drain and transfer to the slow cooker pot. Spoon the onion mixture on top, then add the celery and tomatoes. Pour over the hot stock, season to taste, cover and cook on High for 4–5 hours until the lentils are tender.

Stir in the lemon juice and herbs and spoon into bowls. Top with the yogurt and harissa, then scatter with the pomegranate seeds and serve immediately.

For chickpea & lentil tagine, follow the recipe above, adding ½ teaspoon chilli powder with the other spices and using 100 g (3½ oz) Puy lentils and a 400 g (13 oz) can of chickpeas, drained, instead of 200 g (7 oz) lentils. Omit the mint and pomegranate, but stir in 25 g (1 oz) parsley and serve topped with the yogurt and harissa. **Calories per serving 256**

hoppin' john rice

Calories per serving **292**
Serves **4**
Preparation time **15 minutes,
 plus soaking**
Cooking time **1½–2 hours**

200 g (7 oz) **white basmati
 rice**, soaked in cold water for
 10 minutes
4 **spring onions**, chopped
1 **red pepper**, cored,
 deseeded and diced
150 g (5 oz) peeled **pumpkin**
 or **butternut squash**, cut
 into 1 cm (½ inch) dice
2 **tomatoes**, diced
400 g (13 oz) can **black-eye
 beans**, drained
leaves from 2 **thyme sprigs**
½–1 **red chilli**, deseeded
½ teaspoon **ground allspice**
½ teaspoon **salt**
750 ml (1¼ pints) boiling
 water
15 g (½ oz) **fresh coriander**,
 finely chopped
pepper

Preheat the slow cooker if necessary. Place the soaked rice in a sieve and rinse under cold running water. Drain and place in the slow cooker pot with the spring onions, red pepper, pumpkin or butternut squash, tomatoes, beans, thyme and chilli, to taste.

Stir the allspice and salt into the boiling water and pour over the rice. Season generously with black pepper. Cover and cook on High for 1½–2 hours until the rice is tender and has absorbed the water, stirring once during cooking and adding a little more hot water if the rice is too dry. Add the coriander and fluff up the rice with a fork before serving.

For pumpkin rice, place the soaked and rinsed rice in the slow cooker pot with the spring onions, 375 g (12 oz) peeled and diced pumpkin, 2 chopped garlic cloves, leaves from 2 thyme sprigs, 2.5 cm (1 inch) piece of fresh root ginger, grated, and ½–1 red chilli. Pour over 750 ml (1¼ pints) hot water, season generously and cook as above. Stir in the chopped coriander just before serving. **Calories per serving 248**

moroccan meatballs

Calories per serving **245 (not including the cous cous)**
Serves **4**
Preparation time **30 minutes**
Cooking time **6¼–8¼ hours**

500 g (1 lb) **minced turkey breast**
100 g (3½ oz) drained canned **green lentils**
1 **egg yolk**
1 tablespoon **olive oil**
1 **onion**, sliced
2 **garlic cloves**, finely chopped
1 teaspoon **ground turmeric**
1 teaspoon **ground coriander**
½ teaspoon **ground cumin**
½ teaspoon **ground cinnamon**
2.5 cm (1 inch) piece of **fresh root ginger**, finely chopped
400 g (13 oz) can **chopped tomatoes**
150 ml (¼ pint) **chicken stock**
salt and **pepper**

Preheat the slow cooker if necessary. Place the turkey in a bowl with the lentils and egg yolk, season to taste and mix well. Shape the mixture into 20 small balls using wetted hands.

Heat the oil in a large frying pan over a high heat, add the meatballs and cook, stirring, until browned but not cooked through. Transfer to the slow cooker pot using a slotted spoon. Add the onion to the pan and cook over a medium heat for 5 minutes until softened, then stir in the garlic, spices and ginger and cook for 1 minute.

Stir in the tomatoes and stock, season to taste and bring to the boil, stirring. Pour over the meatballs, cover and cook on Low for 6–8 hours or until the meatballs are cooked through. Stir, then spoon into shallow bowls and serve with lemon couscous, if liked.

For lemon couscous, to serve as an accompaniment, place 200 g (7 oz) couscous in a large bowl with 450 ml (¾ pint) boiling water, the grated rind and juice of 1 lemon and 2 tablespoons olive oil. Season to taste, cover and leave to stand for 5 minutes. Fluff up with a fork and stir in a small bunch of chopped coriander. **Calories per serving 240**

carrot & cumin soup

Calories per serving **235**
Serves **4**
Preparation time **20 minutes**
Cooking time **7–8 hours**

1 tablespoon **sunflower oil**
1 large **onion**, chopped
625 g (1¼ lb) **carrots**, thinly sliced
1½ teaspoons **cumin seeds**, roughly crushed
1 teaspoon **ground turmeric**
50 g (2 oz) **long-grain rice**
1.2 litres (2 pints) **vegetable stock**
salt and **pepper**

To serve
150 ml (¼ pint) **natural yogurt**
4 teaspoons **mango chutney**
4 ready-to-serve **poppadums**

Preheat the slow cooker if necessary. Heat the oil in a large frying pan over a medium heat, add the onion and cook, stirring, for 5 minutes until softened. Stir in the carrots, cumin seeds and turmeric and cook for 2–3 minutes until the onions start to colour.

Stir in the rice, then add the stock, season to taste and bring to the boil. Pour into the slow cooker pot, cover and cook on Low for 7–8 hours or until the carrots are tender.

Purée the soup in a liquidizer or with a hand-held stick blender until smooth, then adjust the seasoning if necessary and ladle the soup into bowls. Top with spoonfuls of yogurt and a little mango chutney and serve with the poppadums.

For spiced parsnip soup, follow the recipe above, replacing the carrots with 625 g (1¼ lb) halved and thinly sliced parsnips. Use 1 teaspoon ground cumin, 1 teaspoon ground coriander and a 3.5 cm (1½ inch) piece of fresh root ginger, finely chopped, instead of the cumin seeds. Continue as above and serve with the yogurt, mango chutney and poppadums. **Calories per serving 275**

cajun red bean soup

Calories per serving **205**
Serves **6**
Preparation time **25 minutes, plus soaking**
Cooking time **8½–10½ hours**

125 g (4 oz) **dried red kidney beans**, soaked overnight in cold water
2 tablespoons **sunflower oil**
1 large **onion**, chopped
1 **red pepper**, cored, deseeded and diced
1 **carrot**, diced
1 **baking potato** 200 g (7 oz), diced
2–3 **garlic cloves**, chopped (optional)
2 teaspoons **Cajun spice mix** or ½–1 teaspoon **chilli powder**
400 g (13 oz) can **chopped tomatoes**
1 tablespoon **brown sugar**
1 litre (1¾ pints) hot **vegetable stock**
50 g (2 oz) **okra**, sliced
50 g (2 oz) **green beans**, cut into short lengths
salt and **pepper**

Preheat the slow cooker if necessary. Drain and rinse the soaked beans, place in a saucepan, cover with fresh water and bring to the boil. Boil vigorously for 10 minutes, then drain in a sieve.

Meanwhile, heat the oil in a large frying pan over a medium heat, add the onion and cook for 5 minutes until softened. Add the red pepper, carrot, potato and garlic (if using) and cook for 2–3 minutes. Stir in the Cajun spice, tomatoes and sugar, season generously and bring to the boil.

Transfer the mixture to the slow cooker pot, add the drained beans and hot stock and mix together. Cover and cook on Low for 8–10 hours until the vegetables are tender.

Add the green vegetables, cover again and cook for 30 minutes. Ladle the soup into bowls and serve.

For Hungarian paprika & red bean soup, follow the recipe above, using 1 teaspoon smoked paprika instead of the Cajun spice and omitting the green vegetables. Purée the soup and add a little boiling water if it is too thick. Ladle into soup bowls, top each portion with 2 tablespoons soured cream and a few caraway seeds and serve immediately. **Calories per serving 252**

lamb & barley broth

Calories per serving **239**
Serves **4**
Preparation time **15 minutes**
Cooking time **8–10 hours**

25 g (1 oz) **butter**
1 tablespoon **sunflower oil**
1 **lamb rump chop** or 125 g
   (4 oz) **lamb fillet**, diced
1 **onion**, chopped
1 small **leek**, chopped
500 g (1 lb) mixed **parsnip,
   swede, turnip** and **carrot**,
   cut into small dice
50 g (2 oz) **pearl barley**
1.2 litres (2 pints) **lamb** or
   chicken stock
¼ teaspoon **ground allspice**
2–3 **rosemary sprigs**
salt and **pepper**
chopped **parsley** or **chives**,
   to garnish

Preheat the slow cooker if necessary. Heat the butter and oil in a large frying pan over a high heat, add the lamb, onion and leek and cook, stirring, for 5 minutes until the lamb is lightly browned.

Stir in the root vegetables and barley, then add the stock, allspice and rosemary. Season to taste and bring to the boil, stirring. Pour into the slow cooker pot, cover and cook on Low for 8–10 hours or until the barley is tender.

Stir well, taste and adjust the seasoning, if necessary, then ladle the soup into bowls. Garnish with chopped herbs and serve.

For Hungarian chorba, follow the recipe above, adding 1 teaspoon smoked paprika, 50 g (2 oz) long-grain rice and a few sprigs of dill instead of the pearl barley. Stir in 1.2 litres (2 pints) lamb stock, 2 tablespoons red wine vinegar and 1 tablespoon light muscovado sugar. Season to taste, bring to the boil and continue as above. Garnish with chopped dill and serve with rye bread, if liked. **Calories per serving 258**

minestrone soup

Calories per serving **267**
Serves **4**
Preparation time **15 minutes**
Cooking time **6½–8¾ hours**

1 tablespoon **olive oil**
1 **onion**, chopped
1 **carrot**, diced
2 **smoked streaky bacon
    rashers**, chopped
2 **garlic cloves**, finely chopped
4 **tomatoes**, skinned and
    chopped
2 **celery sticks**, diced
2 small **courgettes**, diced
3 teaspoons **ready-made
    pesto**, plus 1 extra teaspoon
    to serve
1.2 litres (2 pints) **chicken** or
    vegetable stock
75 g (3 oz) **purple sprouting
    broccoli**, cut into small
    pieces
40 g (1½ oz) tiny **soup pasta**
salt and **pepper**
4 tablespoons freshly grated
    Parmesan cheese, to serve

Preheat the slow cooker if necessary. Heat the oil in a large frying pan over a high heat, add the onion, carrot and bacon and cook for 5 minutes, until lightly browned. Add the garlic, then stir in the tomatoes, celery and courgettes and cook for 1–2 minutes. Stir in the pesto and stock, season to taste and bring to the boil, stirring.

Pour into the slow cooker pot, cover and cook on Low for 6–8 hours or until the vegetables are tender. Add the broccoli and pasta, cover again and cook on High for 15–30 minutes or until the pasta is tender.

Stir well, taste and adjust the seasoning, if necessary, then ladle the soup into bowls. Drizzle each bowl with ½ teaspoon of pesto, to taste. Sprinkle with the grated Parmesan and serve.

For curried vegetable & chicken soup, follow the recipe above, using 2 diced boneless, skinless chicken thighs instead of the bacon and 3 teaspoons mild curry paste instead of the pesto. Add 40 g (1½ oz) basmati rice with 1.2 litres (2 pints) chicken stock and continue as above, omitting the pasta. Garnish with chopped fresh coriander and serve with warm naan bread, if liked.
Calories per serving 255

chunky beef & barley bro

Calories per serving **233**
Serves **4**
Preparation time **15 minutes**
Cooking time **5¼–6¼ hours**

300 g (10 oz) **lean stewing beef**, diced
250 g (8 oz) **swede**, finely diced
250 g (8 oz) **carrot**, finely diced
1 **onion**, finely chopped
50 g (2 oz) **pearl barley**
50 g (2 oz) **dried red lentils**
900 ml (1½ pints) hot **beef stock**
1 teaspoon **dried mixed herbs**
1 teaspoon **mustard powder**
1 tablespoon **Worcestershire sauce**
125 g (4 oz) **green cabbage**, thinly shredded
salt and **pepper**

Preheat the slow cooker if necessary. Place the beef, swede, carrot and onion in the slow cooker pot, then add the pearl barley and lentils.

Mix the hot stock with the herbs, mustard powder and Worcestershire sauce, then pour over the meat and vegetables. Stir well, season to taste, cover and cook on High for 5–6 hours until the beef and barley are tender.

Stir, then add the cabbage. Cover again and cook for 15 minutes until the cabbage is just tender. Ladle into bowls and serve.

For chicken & barley bro, follow the recipe above, using 300 g (10 oz) boneless, skinless diced chicken thighs and 1 sliced leek instead of the beef and onion. Use 900 ml (1½ pints) chicken stock instead of the beef stock, and 50 g (2 oz) diced stoned prunes instead of the Worcestershire sauce. Cook as above, adding the cabbage for the last 15 minutes. **Calories per serving 243**

coconut & rose rice pudding

Calories per serving **231**
Serves **4**
Preparation time **10 minutes**
Cooking time **2½–3 hours**

65 g (2½ oz) **pudding rice**, rinsed in cold water and drained
50 g (2 oz) **caster sugar**
25 g (1 oz) **desiccated coconut**
600 ml (1 pint) **semi-skimmed milk**
½–1 teaspoon **rose water**, to taste

To serve
125 g (4 oz) **raspberries**
2 teaspoons **desiccated coconut**

Preheat the slow cooker if necessary. Place the rice, sugar and coconut in the slow cooker pot, add the milk and stir well. Cover and cook on High for 2½–3 hours until the rice is tender.

Stir well, then add the rose water, to taste. Spoon into bowls, top with the raspberries and a little extra coconut and serve immediately.

For vanilla & orange rice pudding, split 1 vanilla pod lengthways and scrape out the seeds with a small knife. Follow the recipe above, adding the vanilla seeds to the rice and milk in the slow cooker pot with the vanilla pod and the finely grated rind of ½ orange. Stir well, cover and cook as above. Stir again and remove the vanilla pod before serving with raspberries and a sprinkling of coconut. **Calories per serving 233**

sherried bread & butter puddings

Calories per serving **204**
Serves **4**
Preparation time **20 minutes**
Cooking time **3½–4 hours**

50 g (2 oz) **mixed dried fruit**
2 tablespoons **sweet** or **dry sherry**
1 tablespoon **sunflower margarine**
100 g (3½ oz) **white bread slices**
6 teaspoons **caster sugar**
200 ml (7 fl oz) **skimmed milk**
1 teaspoon **vanilla extract**
2 **eggs**

Preheat the slow cooker if necessary. Place the dried fruit and sherry in a small saucepan and bring just to the boil. Remove from the heat and set aside.

Grease 4 x 200 ml (7 fl oz) heatproof dishes with a little margarine, then use the rest to spread on the bread. Cut the bread into cubes, then layer in the dishes with the sherried fruit and 4 teaspoons of the sugar.

Beat the milk, vanilla and eggs in a jug, then strain into the dishes. Cover with squares of greased foil and stand in the slow cooker pot. Pour hot water into the pot to come halfway up the sides of the dishes, then cover and cook on Low for 3½–4 hours or until the custard has set.

Sprinkle the tops of the puddings with the remaining sugar and brown with a cook's blow torch, or under a preheated hot grill. Serve warm.

For Paddington puddings, spread 100 g (3½ oz) white bread slices with 1 tablespoon sunflower margarine and 2 tablespoons reduced-sugar fine-shred marmalade. Layer in the dishes with 50 g (2 oz) dried fruit. Mix the milk, vanilla and eggs, as above, with 2 teaspoons caster sugar and pour over the bread mixture. Cook and finish as above. **Calories per serving 214**

chocolate crème caramels

Calories per serving **251**
Serves **4**
Preparation time **25 minutes, plus cooling and chilling**
Cooking time **3–4 hours**

2 tablespoons **cocoa powder**
2 teaspoons **instant coffee**
2 tablespoons boiling **water**
2 **eggs**
2 **egg yolks**
2 tablespoons **granular sweetener**
450 ml (¾ pint) **semi-skimmed milk**

Caramel
100 g (3½ oz) **granulated sugar**
6 tablespoons cold **water**
2 tablespoons boiling **water**

Preheat the slow cooker if necessary. For the caramel, place the granulated sugar in a heavy-based saucepan with the cold water. Cook over a low heat, without stirring, until the sugar has completely dissolved. Increase the heat and boil for 5–8 minutes or until the syrup turns a rich golden brown, but before it becomes too dark.

Remove the pan from the heat and add the boiling water, taking care as the syrup can spit. Tilt the pan to mix, then pour into 4 x 200 ml (7 fl oz) metal pudding basins. Holding the basins with a cloth, tilt them to swirl the caramel over the base and sides. Cool for 10 minutes.

Place the cocoa, coffee and boiling water in a mixing bowl and stir to a smooth paste. Add the eggs, egg yolks and sweetener and stir until smooth.

Pour the milk into the empty caramel pan and bring just to the boil. Gradually whisk it into the cocoa mixture, then strain through a sieve into a jug. Pour into the basins, cover the tops with greased foil and put in the slow cooker pot.

Pour boiling water into the slow cooker pot to come halfway up the sides of the basins, cover and cook on Low for 3–4 hours until set. Remove from the slow cooker and leave to cool, then chill in the refrigerator for 3–4 hours or overnight. To serve, dip the moulds in hot water, count to 10, loosen the edges with a round-bladed knife, then turn out onto shallow dishes.

For vanilla crème caramels, follow the recipe above to make the caramel and put it in the basins. Mix 2 eggs with 3 egg yolks, 2 tablespoons granular sweetener and 1 teaspoon vanilla extract. Add the hot milk and continue as above. **Calories per serving 239**

brandied chocolate fondue

Calories per serving **220**
Serves **4**
Preparation time **10 minutes**
Cooking time **¾–1 hour**

100 g (3½ oz) **dark
chocolate**, broken into
pieces
6 tablespoons **skimmed milk**
1 teaspoon **granular
sweetener**
1 tablespoon **brandy**

To serve
500 g (1 lb) **strawberries**,
halved if large
150 g (5 oz) **raspberries**
1 large **peach**, halved, stoned
and cut into chunks

Preheat the slow cooker if necessary. Place the chocolate, milk and sweetener in a heatproof bowl, cover with a saucer and stand in the slow cooker pot. Pour boiling water into the slow cooker pot to come halfway up the sides of the bowl, cover and cook on High for ¾–1 hour.

Remove the bowl from the slow cooker and stand on a large plate. Stir the fondue until smooth and glossy, then stir in the brandy.

Arrange the strawberries, raspberries and peaches on the plate. Serve with fondue forks or wooden skewers for spearing the fruit and dipping into the fondue.

For white chocolate fondue, place 100 g (3½ oz) white chocolate, broken into pieces, in a heatproof bowl with a few drops of vanilla extract and 6 tablespoons skimmed milk. Cook as above, then stir in 1 tablespoon Kirsch and serve with mixed berries. **Calories per serving 213**

pancakes with fruit compote

Calories per serving **258**
Serves **4**
Preparation time **15 minutes**
Cooking time **2–2½ hours**

300 g (10 oz) ripe **red plums**,
   halved, stoned and diced
1 **dessert apple**, quartered,
   cored and diced
150 g (5 oz) **blackberries**
¼ teaspoon **ground
   cinnamon**, plus extra to
   decorate
1 tablespoon **granular
   sweetener**
3 tablespoons **water**

Pancakes
75 g (3 oz) **plain flour**
1 **egg** and 1 **egg yolk**
200 ml (7 fl oz) **skimmed milk**
1 teaspoon **sunflower** or
   vegetable oil

To serve
150 g (5 oz) **fromage frais**

Preheat the slow cooker if necessary. Place all the compote ingredients in the slow cooker pot, stir well, cover and cook on High for 2–2½ hours until the fruits have softened.

Make the pancake batter. Place the flour in a large bowl, create a well in the middle and add the egg, egg yolk and milk. Whisk, starting from the centre and gradually drawing the flour into the eggs and milk. Once all the flour is incorporated, beat until you have a smooth, thick batter. Allow to stand for 30 minutes.

Heat a 7-inch frying pan over a moderate heat, wipe it with oiled kitchen paper and ladle some of the pancake batter into the pan, tilting the pan to move the batter around for a thin and even layer. Let cook for at least 30 seconds before flipping the pancake over to cook on the other side. Transfer cooked pancakes to a plate. The batter will make four 7-inch pancakes. Alternatively, use 4 ready-made pancakes, 50 g (2 oz) each.

Warm the pancakes and divide between 4 serving plates. Top with the fruit compote, then fold the pancakes in half and spoon the fromage frais on top. Sprinkle with a little extra cinnamon and serve immediately.

For orchard fruit sundaes, follow the recipe above to make the fruit compote and leave to cool. Spoon into 4 glasses, top with 250 g (8 oz) fromage frais and drizzle each portion with 2 teaspoons maple syrup. **Calories per serving 163**

recipes
under 400
calories

all-in-one chicken casserole

Calories per serving **398**
Serves **4**
Preparation time **20 minutes**
Cooking time **8¼–10¼ hours**

low-calorie cooking oil spray
4 skinless **chicken legs**,
   875 g (1¾ lb) in total
50 g (2 oz) **smoked back**
   bacon, trimmed of fat and
   chopped
300 g (10 oz) **baby new**
   potatoes, thickly sliced
2 small **leeks**, thickly sliced
2 **celery sticks**, thickly sliced
2 **carrots**, sliced
2 teaspoons **plain flour**
1 teaspoon **dried mixed**
   herbs
1 teaspoon **mustard powder**
450 ml (¾ pint) **chicken stock**
50 g (2 oz) **curly kale**, sliced
salt and **pepper**

Spray a large frying pan with a little low-calorie cooking oil spray and place over a high heat until hot. Add the chicken and cook for 5 minutes, turning, until browned all over. Transfer to the slow cooker pot.

Add the bacon and potatoes to the frying pan with a little extra low-calorie cooking oil spray and cook for 4–5 minutes, stirring, until the bacon is beginning to brown. Stir in the white leek slices (reserving the green slices), the celery and carrots. Add the flour, herbs and mustard and stir well.

Pour in the stock, season to taste and bring to the boil, stirring. Spoon over the chicken, cover and cook on Low for 8–10 hours or until the chicken is thoroughly cooked and the meat juices run clear when the thickest parts of the leg are pierced with a sharp knife.

Add the reserved green leek slices and the kale to the slow cooker pot, cover and cook for 15 minutes until the vegetables are just tender. Serve in shallow bowls.

For chicken hotpot, follow the main recipe to make the chicken mixture, omitting the new potatoes and carrots. Transfer to the slow cooker pot and cover with 300 g (10 oz) scrubbed and thinly sliced baking potatoes and 2 thinly sliced carrots, arranging the slices alternately overlapping. Spray with low-calorie cooking oil spray, season to taste, then cook as above. After cooking, brown the top under the grill, if liked. **Calories per serving 403**

beetroot & caraway risotto

Calories per serving **325**
Serves **4**
Preparation time **15 minutes**
Cooking time **5–6 hours**

200 g (7 oz) **long-grain
    brown rice**
300 g (10 oz) **beetroot**, diced
1 **red onion**, finely chopped
2 **garlic cloves**, finely chopped
1 teaspoon **caraway seeds**
2 teaspoons **tomato purée**
1.2 litres (2 pints) hot
    vegetable stock
salt and **pepper**

To serve
4 tablespoons **Greek yogurt**
125 g (4 oz) **smoked salmon
    slices**
handful of **rocket leaves**

Preheat the slow cooker if necessary. Place the rice in a sieve, rinse well under cold running water and drain well.

Place the beetroot, onion and garlic in the slow cooker pot, add the drained rice, caraway seeds and tomato purée, then stir in the hot stock and season generously. Cover and cook on Low for 5–6 hours until the rice and beetroot are tender.

Stir the risotto, spoon on to plates and top each portion with a spoonful of yogurt, some smoked salmon and a few rocket leaves. Serve immediately.

For pumpkin & sage risotto, place 300 g (10 oz) diced pumpkin in the slow cooker pot with 1 finely chopped white onion and 2 chopped garlic cloves. Mix in 250 g (8 oz) rinsed brown rice and flavour with 2 sage sprigs, 1 teaspoon paprika and 2 teaspoons tomato purée. Add 1.2 litres (2 pints) hot vegetable stock, season and cook as above. Serve sprinkled with 75 g (3 oz) finely grated Parmesan cheese. **Calories per serving 354**

cidered gammon hotpot

Calories per serving **375**
Serves **4**
Preparation time **25 minutes**
Cooking time **6–7 hours**

500 g (1 lb) **unsmoked
  gammon joint**, trimmed
  of fat
625 g (1¼ lb) **baking
  potatoes**, cut into 2 cm
  (¾ inch) chunks
200 g (7 oz) small **shallots**,
  peeled
3 **carrots**, thickly sliced
2 **celery sticks**, thickly sliced
1 large **leek**, thickly sliced
2 **bay leaves**
200 ml (7 fl oz) **dry cider**
200 ml (7 fl oz) hot **chicken
  stock**
¼ teaspoon **cloves**
1 teaspoon **mustard powder**
pepper
3 tablespoons chopped
  chives, to garnish

Preheat the slow cooker if necessary. Rinse the gammon joint with cold water and place in the slow cooker pot with the potatoes. Arrange the shallots, carrots, celery and leek slices around the gammon, then tuck in the bay leaves.

Pour the cider and stock into a saucepan, add the cloves and mustard powder, then season with pepper (gammon joints can be salty so don't be tempted to add salt). Bring to the boil, then pour around the gammon. Cover and cook on High for 6–7 hours until the gammon is cooked through.

Cut the gammon into pieces and serve in shallow bowls with the vegetables and stock, garnished with chopped chives.

For gammon in cola, follow the recipe above, using 450 ml (¾ pint) diet cola instead of the cider and stock and omitting the potatoes. Serve with 625 g (1¼ lb) boiled baby new potatoes and 150 g (5 oz) steamed green beans. **Calories per serving 376**

vegetable moussaka

Calories per serving **322**
Serves **4**
Preparation time **25 minutes**
Cooking time **7–9½ hours**

low-calorie cooking oil spray
1 **onion**, roughly chopped
1 large **aubergine**, sliced
2 **garlic cloves**, finely chopped
1 **red pepper**, cored,
    deseeded and cut into
    chunks
1 **yellow pepper**, cored,
    deseeded and cut into
    chunks
2 large **courgettes**, thickly
    sliced
500 g (1 lb) **passata**
150 ml (¼ pint) **vegetable**
    stock
75 g (3 oz) **dried Puy lentils**
leaves from 3 **rosemary**
    sprigs, chopped
1 teaspoon **granular**
    sweetener
salt and **pepper**

Topping
250 ml (8 fl oz) **0% fat Greek**
    yogurt
3 **eggs**
25 g (1 oz) grated **Parmesan**

Preheat the slow cooker if necessary. Spray a large frying pan with a little low-calorie cooking oil spray and place over a high heat until hot. Add the onion and aubergine and fry for 4–5 minutes, stirring until just beginning to brown. Add the garlic, peppers and courgettes and cook for 2 minutes more, then add the passata, stock and lentils.

Add the rosemary and sweetener and season to taste. Bring to the boil, stirring, then transfer to the slow cooker pot. Cover and cook on Low for 6–8 hours until the lentils are tender.

Mix the yogurt, eggs and a little pepper together in a bowl until smooth. Stir the vegetable mixture, then smooth the surface with the back of a spoon. Pour the yogurt mixture over the top in an even layer and sprinkle with the Parmesan. Cover and continue cooking for 45 minutes–1¼ hours until the custard has set.

Place the slow cooker pot under a preheated hot grill for 4–5 minutes until the top is golden, then serve with a green salad, if liked.

For penne with Mediterranean vegetables, make and cook the vegetable and lentil mixture as above. Cook 90 g (3¼ oz) dried wholewheat penne pasta in a saucepan of lightly salted boiling water according to packet instructions. Drain and stir into the cooked vegetables, spoon into shallow dishes and sprinkle with 25 g (1 oz) grated Parmesan cheese. **Calories per serving 399**

oriental pork with pak choi

Calories per serving **387**
Serves **4**
Preparation time **20 minutes**
Cooking time **6¼–7¼ hours**

4 **pork medallions**, 350 g
  (11½ oz) in total
1 **red onion**, thinly sliced
2.5 cm (1 inch) piece of **fresh
  root ginger**, thinly sliced
1 **garlic clove**, thinly sliced
small handful of **fresh
  coriander leaves**
¼ teaspoon **dried chilli flakes**
2 small **star anise**
1 teaspoon **Thai fish sauce**
2 teaspoons **tomato purée**
4 teaspoons **dark soy sauce**
350 ml (12 fl oz) hot **chicken
  stock**
200 g (7 oz) **pak choi**, thickly
  sliced
100 g (3½ oz) **asparagus tips**
250 g (8 oz) **dried egg
  noodles**, to serve

Preheat the slow cooker if necessary. Place the pork medallions in the slow cooker pot in a single layer and scatter with the onion, ginger and garlic. Sprinkle half the coriander leaves on top.

Stir the chilli flakes, star anise, fish sauce, tomato purée and soy sauce into the hot chicken stock, then pour over the pork. Cover and cook on Low for 6–7 hours until the pork is tender.

Add the pak choi and asparagus to the slow cooker pot, cover and cook on High for 15 minutes until the vegetables are just tender and still bright green.

Meanwhile, cook the egg noodles in a saucepan of lightly salted boiling water according to packet instructions until tender. Drain and divide between 4 bowls, top with the pork and vegetables, then spoon over the broth and serve garnished with the remaining coriander.

For oriental pork with mixed vegetables, follow the recipe above, adding 300 g (10 oz) ready-prepared mixed stir-fry vegetables instead of the pak choi and asparagus. **Calories per serving 409**

shakshuka

Calories per serving **314**
Serves **4**
Preparation time **20 minutes**
Cooking time **3½–4½ hours**

low-calorie cooking oil spray
2 **red onions**, roughly
  chopped
75 g (3 oz) **chorizo**, diced
625 g (1¼ lb) **tomatoes**,
  chopped
½ teaspoon **dried chilli flakes**
1 tablespoon **tomato purée**
2 teaspoons **granular**
  sweetener
2 teaspoons **paprika**
1 teaspoon **dried oregano**
4 **eggs**
salt and **pepper**

To serve
chopped **parsley**
4 small slices of **wholemeal**
  bread, toasted

Preheat the slow cooker if necessary. Spray a large frying pan with a little low-calorie cooking oil spray and place over a medium heat until hot. Add the onion and chorizo and cook for 5 minutes, stirring until the onion has softened.

Add the chopped tomatoes, chilli flakes, tomato purée, sweetener, paprika and oregano and season to taste. Transfer the mixture to the slow cooker pot, cover and cook on High for 3–4 hours until the tomatoes have softened and the sauce is thick.

Make 4 indents in the tomato mixture with the back of a dessert spoon, then break an egg into each one. Cover again and cook for 15 minutes or until the eggs are set to your liking. Sprinkle with a little chopped parsley, then spoon on to plates and serve with toast.

For mixed vegetable shakshuka, follow the recipe above, omitting the chorizo and using just 1 chopped red onion. Add 1 diced red pepper, 1 large diced courgette, and 2 finely chopped garlic cloves to the frying pan with the onion and continue as above.
Calories per serving 205

beef bourguignon

Calories per serving **317 (not including rice)**
Serves **4**
Preparation time **20 minutes**
Cooking time **10–11 hours**

low-calorie cooking oil spray
625 g (1 ¼ lb) **stewing beef**, trimmed of fat and cubed
100 g (3½ oz) **bacon**, diced
300 g (10 oz) small **shallots**, peeled
3 **garlic cloves**, finely chopped
1 tablespoon **plain flour**
150 ml (¼ pint) **red wine**
300 ml (½ pint) **beef stock**
1 tablespoon **tomato purée**
small bunch of **mixed herbs** or a **dried bouquet garni**
salt and **pepper**
chopped **parsley**, to garnish

Preheat the slow cooker if necessary. Spray a large frying pan with a little low-calorie cooking oil spray and place over a high heat until hot. Add the beef, a few pieces at a time until all the beef is in the pan, and cook for 5 minutes, stirring, until browned. Use a slotted spoon to transfer the beef to the slow cooker pot.

Add the bacon and shallots to the frying pan and cook over a medium heat for 2–3 minutes until the bacon is just beginning to brown. Stir in the garlic and flour, then add the wine, stock, tomato purée and herbs. Season to taste and bring to the boil, stirring.

Pour the sauce over the beef, cover and cook on Low for 10–11 hours until the beef is tender. Stir, garnish with chopped parsley and serve with rice, if liked.

For beef goulash, follow the recipe above, adding 2 teaspoons mild paprika, 1 teaspoon caraway seeds, ¼ teaspoon ground cinnamon and ¼ teaspoon ground allspice instead of the herbs. **Calories per serving 319**

slow-cooked greek lamb

Calories per serving **353**
Serves **4**
Preparation time **20 minutes**
Cooking time **9¼–10½ hours**

low-calorie cooking oil spray
4 **lean lamb leg steaks**,
   125 g (4 oz) each
1 large **onion**, thinly sliced
2 **garlic cloves**, finely chopped
1 **lemon**, diced
250 g (8 oz) **tomatoes**,
   roughly chopped
2 teaspoons **coriander seeds**,
   roughly crushed
1 **bay leaf**
1 teaspoon **granular**
   sweetener
1 tablespoon **sun-dried**
   tomato paste
300 ml (½ pint) **lamb stock**
300 g (10 oz) **baby new**
   potatoes, thickly sliced
300 g (10 oz) **courgettes**,
   diced
salt and **pepper**
2 tablespoons chopped
   parsley, to garnish

Preheat the slow cooker if necessary. Spray a large frying pan with a little low-calorie cooking oil spray and place over a high heat until hot. Add the lamb steaks and cook for 4–5 minutes, turning once, until browned on both sides. Transfer to a plate.

Add the onion to the frying pan and cook for 4–5 minutes until softened, then add the garlic, lemon and tomatoes. Add the coriander seeds, bay leaf, sweetener, tomato paste and lamb stock, season to taste and bring to the boil.

Arrange the potatoes over the base of the slow cooker pot, then place the lamb steaks in a single layer on top. Pour over the hot stock mixture, cover and cook on Low for 9–10 hours until the lamb and potatoes are tender.

Add the courgettes, cover again and cook on High for 15–30 minutes until tender. Spoon into shallow bowls, sprinkle with the parsley and serve immediately.

For slow-cooked lamb with rosemary, follow the recipe above, adding 3 rosemary sprigs instead of the lemon, coriander seeds and bay leaf. Cook as above, adding the courgettes at the end. Serve garnished with the parsley. **Calories per serving 352**

tarragon chicken with mushrooms

Calories per serving **319**

Serves **4**

Preparation time **20 minutes**

Cooking time **8¼–9½ hours**

low-calorie cooking oil spray

4 skinless **chicken legs**,
  1.2 kg (2 lb 6 oz) in total

2 **leeks**, sliced

175 g (6 oz) **closed-cap
  mushrooms**, sliced

1 tablespoon **plain flour**

1 teaspoon **mustard powder**

450 ml (¾ pint) **chicken stock**

2 tablespoons chopped
  tarragon, plus extra to
  garnish

3 tablespoons **sherry**
  (optional)

125 g (4 oz) **fine green beans**

salt and **pepper**

Preheat the slow cooker if necessary. Spray a large frying pan with a little low-calorie cooking oil spray and place over a high heat until hot. Add the chicken legs and cook for 4–5 minutes, turning once, until golden. Transfer to the slow cooker pot.

Add a little extra low-calorie cooking oil spray to the pan if necessary, then add the white leek slices (reserving the green slices) and the mushrooms and cook for 2–3 minutes. Stir in the flour, then add the mustard powder, stock, tarragon and sherry, if using. Season to taste and bring to the boil, stirring.

Pour the liquid and vegetables over the chicken, cover and cook on Low for 8–9 hours until the chicken is tender and cooked through.

Stir the casserole, then add the remaining green leek slices and the green beans. Cover again and cook on High for 15–30 minutes until the vegetables are tender. Spoon into shallow bowls and serve garnished with a little extra tarragon.

For low-cal garlicky mash, to serve as an accompaniment, peel and cut 625 g (1¼ lb) potatoes into chunks and cook in a saucepan of lightly salted boiling water for about 15 minutes until tender. Drain and mash with 3 tablespoons chicken stock, 2 crushed garlic cloves and a little salt and pepper. **Calories per serving 122**

venison sausages with red cabbage

Calories per serving **354**
Serves **4**
Preparation time **20 minutes**
Cooking time **5–6 hours**

8 **venison sausages**,
   525 g (1 lb 1 oz) in total
low-calorie cooking oil spray
1 **onion**, chopped
150 ml (¼ pint) **red wine**
600 ml (1 pint) **beef stock**
2 tablespoons **cranberry**
   sauce
1 tablespoon **tomato purée**
2 **bay leaves**
300 g (10 oz) **potatoes**, cut
   into 2.5 cm (1 inch) chunks
2 **carrots**, cut into 2 cm
   (¾ inch) chunks
250 g (8 oz) **tomatoes**,
   roughly chopped
250 g (8 oz) **red cabbage**,
   finely shredded
125 g (4 oz) **dried green**
   lentils
salt and **pepper**

Preheat the slow cooker if necessary. Cook the sausages under a preheated medium grill for 5 minutes, turning until browned but not cooked through.

Meanwhile, spray a large frying pan with a little low-calorie cooking oil spray and place over a medium heat until hot. Add the onion and cook for 4–5 minutes until just softened. Add the red wine, stock, cranberry sauce, tomato purée and bay leaves, then season to taste and bring to the boil, stirring.

Place the potatoes and carrots in the slow cooker pot with the tomatoes, red cabbage and lentils on top. Pour over the hot wine mixture, then add the sausages and press down into the liquid. Cover and cook on High for 5–6 hours until the sausages and potatoes are cooked through and the lentils are tender. Serve in shallow bowls.

For braised lamb shanks with red cabbage, omit the venison sausages and brown 4 small lamb shanks, 750 g (1 ½ lb) in total, in a little low-calorie cooking oil spray in a frying pan, then continue with the recipe above. **Calories per serving 335**

mushroom & wheatberry pilau

Calories per serving **316**
Serves **4**
Preparation time **20 minutes**
Cooking time **3½–4 hours**

1 tablespoon **olive oil**
1 **onion**, thinly sliced
2 **garlic cloves**, finely chopped
325 ml (11 fl oz) **brown ale**
450 ml (¾ pint) **vegetable stock**
3 **sage sprigs**
¼ teaspoon grated **nutmeg**
5 cm (2 inch) **cinnamon stick**
1 tablespoon **sun-dried tomato paste**
200 g (7 oz) **wheatberries**
250 g (8 oz) **chestnut mushrooms**, halved
250 g (8 oz) large **closed-cap mushrooms**, quartered
salt and **pepper**
15 g (½ oz) **parsley**, roughly chopped, to garnish

Preheat the slow cooker if necessary. Heat the oil in a large frying pan over a medium heat until hot. Add the onion and fry for 4–5 minutes, stirring until just beginning to soften. Add the garlic, brown ale, stock, sage, nutmeg and cinnamon. Stir in the tomato paste and season well, then bring to the boil.

Place the wheatberries and mushrooms in the slow cooker pot. Pour over the hot ale mixture, then cover and cook on High for 3½–4 hours until the wheatberries are tender and nearly all the liquid has been absorbed. Stir well, then sprinkle with the parsley. Spoon into shallow bowls to serve.

For red pepper wheatberry pilau, fry 1 sliced red onion in the oil as above, then add 2 finely chopped garlic cloves and 2 cored, deseeded and sliced red peppers. Stir in 200 ml (7 fl oz) red wine, 600 ml (1 pint) vegetable stock, a small handful of basil leaves and 1 tablespoon sun-dried tomato paste. Season to taste and bring to the boil, then pour over the wheatberries in the slow cooker pot and cook as above. **Calories per serving 363**

three-fish gratin

Calories per serving **395**
Serves **4**
Preparation time **20 minutes**
Cooking time **2¼–3¼ hours**

2 tablespoons **cornflour**
400 ml (14 fl oz) **skimmed milk**
50 g (2 oz) **mature Cheddar cheese**, grated
3 tablespoons chopped **parsley**
1 **leek**, thinly sliced
1 **bay leaf**
500 g (1 lb) **mixed fish**, diced (such as salmon, cod and smoked haddock)
salt and **pepper**

Topping
20 g (¾ oz) **fresh breadcrumbs**
40 g (1½ oz) **mature Cheddar cheese**, grated

To serve
325 g (11 oz) each of **peas** and **mangetout**, steamed

Preheat the slow cooker if necessary. Place the cornflour in a saucepan with a little of the milk and mix to a smooth paste. Stir in the rest of the milk, then add the cheese, parsley, leek and bay leaf. Season to taste and bring to the boil, stirring until thickened.

Place the fish in the slow cooker pot. Pour over the hot leek sauce, cover and cook on Low for 2–3 hours until the fish is cooked through.

Transfer the fish mixture to a shallow ovenproof dish, sprinkle the breadcrumbs and cheese over the top, then place under a preheated hot grill for 4–5 minutes until golden brown. Serve with the steamed peas and mangetout.

For fish pies, follow the recipe above, omitting the breadcrumb and cheese topping. Peel and cut 625 g (1¼ lb) potatoes into chunks. Cook the potatoes in a saucepan of lightly salted boiling water for 15 minutes or until tender. Drain and mash with 4 tablespoons skimmed milk, then season and stir in 40 g (1½ oz) grated mature Cheddar cheese. Divide the cooked fish mixture between 4 individual pie dishes, spoon over the mash, rough up the top with a fork, then brush with 1 beaten egg. Cook under a preheated medium grill until golden. **Calories per serving 435**

thai fish curry

Calories per serving **326**
Serves **4**
Preparation time **15 minutes**
Cooking time **2¼–3¼ hours**

1 **onion**, quartered
15 g (½ oz) **fresh coriander leaves** and **stalks**, plus extra to garnish
2.5 cm (1 inch) piece of **fresh root ginger**, sliced
1 **lemon grass stalk**, thickly sliced, or 1 teaspoon **lemon grass paste**
200 ml (7 fl oz) **light coconut milk**
200 ml (7 fl oz) **fish stock**
1 teaspoon **Thai fish sauce**
1 tablespoon **Thai red curry paste**
4 **salmon steaks**, 500 g (1 lb) in total
low-calorie cooking oil spray
400 g (13 oz) **ready-prepared stir-fry vegetables**
grated rind and juice of **1 lime**

Preheat the slow cooker if necessary. Place the onion, coriander, ginger and lemon grass in a food processor and blitz until finely chopped. Transfer to a medium saucepan and stir in the coconut milk, stock, fish sauce and curry paste. This mixture can be chilled until ready to use.

Arrange the salmon steaks in the base of the slow cooker pot. Bring the coconut mixture to the boil, stirring, then pour over the salmon. Cover and cook on Low for 2–3 hours until the salmon flakes easily when pressed with a small knife.

Spray a large frying pan with a little low-calorie cooking oil spray and place over a high heat until hot. Add the vegetables and cook for 2–3 minutes until piping hot.

Break the salmon into large flakes and stir the lime rind and juice into the curry. Spoon into bowls and top with the vegetables and a little extra coriander.

For Thai vegetable curry, follow the recipe above to make the sauce, using 200 ml (7 fl oz) vegetable stock instead of the fish stock, and omitting the fish sauce if serving the curry to vegetarians. Place a 200 g (7 oz) can of bamboo shoots in the slow cooker pot with 175 g (6 oz) baby corn cobs, 150 g (5 oz) whole cherry tomatoes and 1 diced courgette. Pour over the sauce, cook and serve with stir-fried vegetables as above. **Calories per serving 138**

tangy turkey tagine

Calories per serving **385 (not including naan)**
Serves **4**
Preparation time **25 minutes**
Cooking time **8–9 hours**

low-calorie cooking oil spray
400 g (13 oz) **turkey breast**, diced
1 **onion**, chopped
2 **garlic cloves**, finely chopped
1 tablespoon **plain flour**
450 ml (¾ pint) **chicken stock**
2 pinches of **saffron strands** or 1 teaspoon **ground turmeric**
5 cm (2 inch) **cinnamon stick**
finely grated rind of 1 **lemon**
400 g (13 oz) can **chickpeas**, drained
25 g (1 oz) **sultanas**
salt and **pepper**

To serve
175 g (6 oz) **couscous**
450 ml (¾ pint) boiling **water**
4 tablespoons chopped **mint** or mixed **mint** and **parsley**

Preheat the slow cooker if necessary. Spray a large frying pan with a little low-calorie cooking oil spray and place over a high heat until hot. Add the turkey, a few pieces at a time until all the turkey is in the pan, and cook for 5 minutes, stirring until golden. Use a slotted spoon to transfer the turkey to a plate.

Add the onion to the frying pan and cook for 4–5 minutes until softened. Stir in the garlic and flour, then add the stock and mix well. Add the saffron or turmeric, cinnamon and lemon rind, then the chickpeas and sultanas. Season to taste and bring to the boil, stirring.

Pour into the slow cooker pot, add the turkey pieces and press into the liquid. Cover and cook on Low for 8–9 hours until the turkey is tender and cooked through.

Meanwhile, place the couscous in a mixing bowl, pour over the boiling water, cover with a plate and leave to soak for 5 minutes until tender. Stir in the chopped herbs, season to taste and fluff up with a fork. Divide the couscous between 4 plates and top with the tagine. Serve with naan, if liked.

For harissa-baked turkey, follow the recipe above, using 300 ml (½ pint) chicken stock and 250 g (8 oz) diced tomatoes instead of 450 ml (¾ pint) chicken stock. Omit the saffron, cinnamon and lemon and add 2 teaspoons harissa paste and 2.5 cm (1 inch) piece of fresh root ginger, chopped, instead. Cook as above and serve with the herby couscous. **Calories per serving 396**

beery beef cheeks

Calories per serving **363**
Serves **4**
Preparation time **20 minutes**
Cooking time **5–6 hours**

1 tablespoon **sunflower oil**
600 g (1 lb 4 oz) **beef cheeks**,
  cut into 4 cm (1½ inch)
  thick slices
2 **red onions**, cut into wedges
250 ml (8 fl oz) **brown ale**
150 ml (¼ pint) **beef stock**
1 tablespoon **tomato purée**
2 teaspoons **cornflour**
2 **rosemary sprigs**
2 **bay leaves**
300 g (10 oz) small
  Chantenay carrots, halved
  lengthways
2 **celery sticks**, thickly sliced
salt and **pepper**

Heat the oil in a large frying pan over a high heat until hot. Add the beef, a few pieces at a time until all the beef is in the pan, and cook for 5 minutes, stirring until browned. Use a slotted spoon to transfer the beef to the slow cooker pot, arranging it in a single layer.

Add the onion to the frying pan and cook for 3–4 minutes until softened. Add the brown ale, stock and tomato purée. Mix the cornflour to a smooth paste with a little cold water and stir into the pan with the herbs. Season to taste and bring to the boil, stirring.

Place the carrots and celery on top of the beef, then pour over the hot beer mixture. Cover and cook on High for 5–6 hours until the beef is very tender. Spoon into shallow bowls and serve with sugar snap peas and frozen peas, if liked.

For beery chestnuts & mushrooms, follow the recipe above, using 500 g (1 lb) whole mixed small mushrooms instead of the beef, and adding 175 g (6 oz) canned chestnuts at the same time as the herbs. **Calories per serving 219**

148

pork stew with sweet potatoes

Calories per serving **315**
Serves **4**
Preparation time **20 minutes**
Cooking time **8¼–9¼ hours**

low-calorie cooking oil spray
500 g (1 lb) **lean pork**, cubed
1 **onion**, chopped
125 g (4 oz) **closed-cap mushrooms**, sliced
450 ml (¾ pint) **chicken stock**
2 tablespoons **tomato purée**
2 tablespoons **soy sauce**
¼ teaspoon **chilli powder**
½ teaspoon **ground allspice**
¼ teaspoon **ground cinnamon**
1 teaspoon **granular sweetener**
150 g (5 oz) **carrots**, thinly sliced
2 **celery sticks**, thickly sliced
375 g (12 oz) **sweet potato**, cut into 2.5 cm (1 inch) chunks
125 g (4 oz) **curly kale**, shredded

Preheat the slow cooker if necessary. Spray a large frying pan with a little low-calorie cooking oil spray and place over a high heat until hot. Add the pork, a few pieces at a time until all the pork is in the pan, and cook for 3 minutes, stirring. Add the onion and cook for a further 2–3 minutes until the pork is golden.

Stir in the mushrooms, then add the stock, tomato purée and soy sauce. Add the chilli powder, allspice, cinnamon and sweetener, season to taste and bring to the boil, stirring.

Place the carrots, celery and sweet potato in the slow cooker pot, then pour over the pork and sauce. Press the meat into the liquid, cover and cook on Low for 8–9 hours until the pork is tender.

Stir the stew, then add the kale. Cover again and cook on High for 15 minutes, then spoon into bowls and serve immediately.

For fragrant sausage & sweet potato stew, place 500 g (1 lb) reduced-fat pork sausages under a preheated hot grill until browned but not cooked through. Transfer to the slow cooker pot. Continue with the recipe above, omitting the pork. **Calories per serving 362**

polish sausage stew

Calories per serving **355**
Serves **4**
Preparation time **20 minutes**
Cooking time **8–10 hours**

low-calorie cooking oil spray
325 g (11 oz) boneless,
  skinless **chicken thighs**,
  cubed
1 **onion**, chopped
2 teaspoons **mild paprika**
1 teaspoon **caraway seeds**
1 **dessert apple**, quartered,
  cored and thinly sliced
250 g (8 oz) **tomatoes**, diced
1 tablespoon **granular**
  sweetener
400 g (13 oz) **sauerkraut**,
  drained
200 g (7 oz) **smoked pork**
  sausage, sliced
100 g (3½ oz) **gherkins**,
  sliced
450 ml (¾ pint) hot **chicken**
  stock
salt and **pepper**

To garnish
3 tablespoons chopped **dill**
3 tablespoons chopped
  parsley

Preheat the slow cooker if necessary. Spray a large frying pan with a little low-calorie cooking oil spray and place over a high heat until hot. Add the chicken, a few pieces at a time until all the chicken is in the pan, then add the onion and cook for 5 minutes, stirring, until the chicken is golden.

Add the paprika, caraway, apple, tomatoes and sweetener to the pan and heat through. Place the sauerkraut in the slow cooker pot and pour the chicken mixture on top, then add the sliced sausage and gherkins.

Pour over the hot stock and season to taste. Stir well, cover and cook on Low for 8–10 hours until the chicken is cooked through. Serve in bowls, garnished with chopped dill and parsley.

For Polish pork stew, follow the recipe above, using 500 g (1 lb) diced lean pork instead of the chicken. Use 1 teaspoon mild paprika and 1 teaspoon smoked hot paprika or chilli powder instead of 2 teaspoons mild paprika, and continue with the recipe, omitting the smoked sausage. **Calories per serving 251**

skinny cassoulet

Calories per serving **364**
Serves **4**
Preparation time **20 minutes**
Cooking time **8–10 hours**

low-calorie cooking oil spray
500 g (1 lb) **lean pork**, diced
75 g (3 oz) **chorizo**, sliced
1 **onion**, chopped
3 **garlic cloves**, finely chopped
1 **red pepper**, cored,
    deseeded and diced
2 **celery sticks**, sliced
1 **carrot**, diced
500 g (1 lb) **passata**
1 teaspoon **dried
    Mediterranean herbs**
2 x 375 g (12 oz) cans
    cannellini beans, drained
3 tablespoons **fresh
    breadcrumbs**
salt and **pepper**

Preheat the slow cooker if necessary. Spray a large frying pan with a little low-calorie cooking oil spray and place over a high heat until hot. Add the pork, a few pieces at a time until all the pork is in the pan, and cook for 5 minutes, stirring, until browned. Use a slotted spoon to transfer the pork to the slow cooker pot.

Add the chorizo and onion to the frying pan and cook for 4–5 minutes until the onion has softened. Stir in the garlic, red pepper, celery, carrot, passata and herbs. Season to taste and bring to the boil, stirring.

Place the beans in the slow cooker pot, pour over the passata mixture and stir well. Level the surface with the back of a spoon, then sprinkle over the breadcrumbs. Cover and cook on Low for 8–10 hours until the pork is tender. Spoon into shallow bowls and serve with salad, if liked.

For chicken cassoulet, follow the recipe above, using 500 g (1 lb) boneless, skinless chicken thighs, diced, instead of the pork. Mix the breadcrumbs with 2 tablespoons chopped rosemary and 2 tablespoons chopped parsley, then spoon over the cassoulet and cook as above. **Calories per serving 346**

feijoada ham

Calories per serving **312**
Serves **4**
Preparation time **20 minutes**
Cooking time **5–6 hours**

1 **onion**, chopped
2 **celery sticks**, thickly sliced
150 g (5 oz) **carrots**, diced
375 g (12 oz) can **black
    beans**, drained
1 **red chilli**, halved and
    deseeded
2 **thyme sprigs**
pared rind of 1 **orange**
500 g (1 lb) **unsmoked
    gammon joint**, trimmed
    of fat
1 teaspoon **mild paprika**
½ teaspoon **ground allspice**
450 ml (¾ pint) hot **vegetable
    stock**
salt and **pepper**
4 tablespoons chopped
    parsley, to garnish

To serve
150 g (5 oz) **rice**

Preheat the slow cooker if necessary. Place the onion, celery and carrot in the slow cooker pot, then add the drained beans, chilli, thyme and orange rind. Nestle the gammon joint in the centre.

Stir the paprika and allspice into the hot stock, then season to taste and pour over the gammon joint. Spoon some of the orange rind and thyme on top of the joint, cover and cook on High for 5–6 hours until the gammon is very tender.

Cook the rice in a saucepan of lightly salted boiling water, according to packet instructions, until tender.

Cut the gammon into pieces, then spoon into shallow bowls with the beans, vegetables and sauce. Sprinkle with the parsley and serve with the rice.

For feijoada chicken, follow the recipe above, using a 1.35 kg (2 lb 10 oz) oven-ready chicken instead of the gammon joint. Cook on High for 5–6 hours or until the chicken is thoroughly cooked and the meat juices run clear when the thickest parts of the leg and breast are pierced with a sharp knife. **Calories per serving 318**

salmon bourride

Calories per serving **336**
Serves **4**
Preparation time **20 minutes**
Cooking time **3–3½ hours**

low-calorie cooking oil spray
1 **onion**, chopped
2 **garlic cloves**, finely chopped
½ **red pepper**, cored,
    deseeded and very thinly
    sliced
½ **orange pepper**, cored,
    deseeded and very thinly
    sliced
400 g (13 oz) can **chopped
    tomatoes**
150 ml (¼ pint) **vegetable
    stock**
1 teaspoon **granular
    sweetener**
1 teaspoon **cornflour**
400 g (13 oz) can **artichoke
    hearts**, drained
4 **salmon steaks**, 140 g
    (4½ oz) each
finely grated rind of 1 **lemon**
½ teaspoon **dried
    Mediterranean herbs**
salt and **pepper**
200 g (7 oz) steamed **green
    beans**, to serve

Preheat the slow cooker if necessary. Spray a large frying pan with a little low-calorie cooking oil spray and place over a high heat until hot. Add the onion, garlic and peppers and cook for 4–5 minutes until softened.

Stir in the tomatoes, stock and sweetener. Mix the cornflour to a smooth paste with a little cold water and stir into the pan. Season to taste and bring to the boil, stirring.

Transfer the mixture into the slow cooker pot, stir in the artichoke hearts, then arrange the salmon steaks in a single layer on top, pressing them down into the liquid. Sprinkle the lemon rind and herbs over the salmon and season lightly.

Cover and cook on Low for 3–3½ hours until the salmon steaks are cooked and flake easily when pressed with a small knife. Spoon into shallow bowls and serve with the steamed green beans.

For squid bourride, rinse 625 g (1¼ lb) prepared squid and take the tentacles out of the tubes. Slice the squid tubes and drain well. Follow the recipe above, using the sliced squid tubes instead of the salmon and cooking on Low for 4–5 hours. Add the squid tentacles and continue cooking for 30 minutes until tender, then serve with the steamed green beans. **Calories per serving 205**

tangy chicken, fennel & leek braise

Calories per serving **316**
Serves **4**
Preparation time **20 minutes**
Cooking time **8½–9½ hours**

low-calorie cooking oil spray
625 g (1¼ lb) boneless,
  skinless **chicken thighs**,
  halved
1 **fennel bulb**, cored and
  sliced, green fronds reserved
2 **leeks**, thinly sliced
350 ml (12 fl oz) **chicken
  stock**
finely grated rind and juice of
  ½ **orange**
2 teaspoons **cornflour**
salt and **pepper**

Preheat the slow cooker if necessary. Spray a large frying pan with a little low-calorie cooking oil spray and place over a high heat until hot. Add the chicken and cook for 3–4 minutes, turning once, until browned on both sides. Use a slotted spoon to transfer to a plate.

Add the fennel and white leek slices to the frying pan, reserving the green slices. Cook for 2–3 minutes until just beginning to soften, then add the stock, and orange rind and juice. Mix the cornflour to a smooth paste with a little cold water and stir into the pan. Season to taste and bring to the boil, stirring.

Transfer the mixture to the slow cooker pot, arrange the chicken pieces on top in a single layer and press into the liquid. Cover and cook on Low for 8–9 hours until the chicken is cooked through.

Add the reserved green leek slices, stir into the sauce, cover again and cook for 30 minutes. Serve garnished with the reserved fennel fronds.

For braised mustard chicken & leeks, follow the recipe above, using 75 g (3 oz) diced lean back bacon instead of the fennel. Use 1 teaspoon Dijon mustard instead of the orange rind and juice and cook as above. Garnish with chopped parsley. **Calories per serving 323**

quorn sausages with onion gravy

Calories per serving **374**
Serves **4**
Preparation time **20 minutes**
Cooking time **4½–5½ hours**

low-calorie cooking oil spray
2 x 240 g (7½ oz) packets of
    soya sausages
300 g (10 oz) **onions**, thinly
    sliced
2 teaspoons **dark muscovado
    sugar**
350 ml (12 fl oz) **vegetable
    stock**
1 tablespoon **tomato purée**
2 teaspoons **wholegrain
    mustard**
2 teaspoons **cornflour**
salt and **pepper**
675 g (1 lb 6 oz) **celeriac**,
    cubed just before cooking
chopped **parsley**, to garnish
    (optional)

To serve
360 g (11¾ oz) **fine green
    beans**, steamed

Preheat the slow cooker if necessary. Spray a large frying pan with a little low-calorie cooking oil spray and place over a high heat until hot. Add the sausages and cook for 2–3 minutes until browned all over. Transfer to the slow cooker pot in a single layer.

Add a little extra low-calorie cooking oil spray to the frying pan, add the onions and cook over a medium heat for 5 minutes until just beginning to soften. Add the sugar and continue to cook for 5 minutes until deep brown, being careful not to burn the onions.

Stir in the stock, tomato purée and mustard. Mix the cornflour to a smooth paste with a little cold water and stir into the pan. Season to taste and bring to the boil, stirring. Pour over the sausages, cover and cook on High for 4–5 hours until the sausages are cooked through.

Cook the celeriac in a saucepan of lightly salted boiling water for 15–20 minutes until tender. Drain and mash the celeriac with 3–4 tablespoons of the cooking water and season to taste. Divide the mash between 4 serving plates and top with the sausages and onion gravy. Sprinkle with a little chopped parsley, if liked, and serve with the steamed green beans.

For pork sausages with onion gravy, grill 8 reduced-fat pork sausages until browned all over but not cooked through and arrange in the slow cooker pot. Follow the recipe above to make the onion gravy, pour over the sausages and cook on High for 5–6 hours until the sausages are cooked through. Serve with celeriac mash and green beans, as above. **Calories per serving 351**

red pepper & chorizo tortilla

Calories per serving **309**
Serves **4**
Preparation time **20 minutes**
Cooking time **2–2½ hours**

1 tablespoon **olive oil**, plus
  extra for greasing
1 small **onion**, chopped
75 g (3 oz) **chorizo**, diced
6 **eggs**
150 ml (¼ pint) **milk**
100 g (3½ oz) **roasted red
  peppers** from a jar, sliced
250 g (8 oz) cooked **potatoes**,
  sliced
salt and **pepper**

Preheat the slow cooker if necessary. Lightly oil a
1.2 litre (2 pint) ovenproof soufflé dish and line the base
with nonstick baking paper. Heat the oil in a small frying
pan over a medium heat, add the onion and chorizo and
cook for 4–5 minutes until the onion has softened.

Beat the eggs and milk together in a mixing bowl and
season to taste. Add the onion and chorizo, red pepper
and potatoes and toss together.

Tip the mixture into the oiled dish, cover the top with foil
and put in the slow cooker pot. Pour boiling water into
the slow cooker pot to come halfway up the sides of the
dish, cover and cook on High for 2–2½ hours until the
egg mixture has just set in the centre.

Loosen the edges of the tortilla with a round-bladed
knife, turn it out on to a plate and peel off the lining
paper. Cut into slices and serve hot or cold, with salad
if liked.

For cheesy bacon & rosemary tortilla, follow
the recipe above, using 75 g (3 oz) diced smoked
streaky bacon instead of the chorizo. Beat the eggs
and milk in a bowl with the chopped leaves from
2 small rosemary sprigs, 4 tablespoons freshly grated
Parmesan or Cheddar cheese and 75 g (3 oz) sliced
button mushrooms. Season to taste and continue as
above. **Calories per serving 282**

smoked cod with bean mash

Calories per serving **308**
Serves **4**
Preparation time **20 minutes**
Cooking time **1½–2 hours**

2 x 400 g (13 oz) cans
  cannellini beans, drained
bunch of **spring onions**, thinly
  sliced
400 ml (14 fl oz) hot **fish**
  stock
1 teaspoon **wholegrain**
  mustard
grated rind and juice of
  1 **lemon**
4 **smoked cod loins**, 625 g
  (1¼ lb) in total
4 tablespoons **crème fraîche**
small bunch of **parsley,**
  watercress or **rocket**
  leaves, roughly chopped
salt and **pepper**

Preheat the slow cooker if necessary. Put the beans into the slow cooker pot with the white spring onion slices (reserving the green slices). Mix the fish stock with the mustard and lemon rind and juice, season to taste and pour into the pot.

Arrange the fish on top and sprinkle with a little extra pepper. Cover and cook on Low for 1½–2 hours or until the fish flakes easily when pressed with a small knife. Transfer the fish to a plate and keep warm.

Pour off nearly all the cooking liquid, then mash the beans roughly. Stir in the crème fraîche, the reserved green spring onion slices and the parsley, watercress or rocket. Adjust the seasoning if necessary, spoon the mash on to 4 plates and top with the fish. Serve immediately.

For baked salmon with basil bean mash, follow the recipe above, omitting the mustard. Use 4 x 150 g (5 oz) salmon steaks instead of the cod and a small bunch of basil instead of the parsley, watercress or rocket leaves. **Calories per serving 451**

mushroom & tomato rigatoni

Calories per serving **385 (not including Parmesan)**
Serves **4**
Preparation time **20 minutes, plus soaking**
Cooking time **2½–3 hours**

250 g (8 oz) **rigatoni** or **pasta quills**
3 tablespoons **olive oil**
1 **onion**, sliced
2–3 **garlic cloves**, finely chopped
250 g (8 oz) **closed-cap mushrooms**, sliced
250 g (8 oz) **portabello mushrooms**, sliced
250 g (8 oz) **tomatoes**, cut into chunks
400 g (13 oz) can **chopped tomatoes**
200 ml (7 fl oz) **vegetable stock**
1 tablespoon **tomato purée**
3 **rosemary sprigs**
salt and **pepper**

Preheat the slow cooker if necessary. Place the pasta in a large bowl, cover with boiling water and leave to stand for 10 minutes.

Heat 1 tablespoon of the oil in a large frying pan over a medium heat, add the onion and cook for 5 minutes, until softened. Stir in the remaining oil, the garlic and mushrooms and cook, stirring, until the mushrooms are just beginning to brown.

Stir in the fresh and canned tomatoes, stock and tomato purée. Add the rosemary, season to taste and bring to the boil.

Drain the pasta and put it in the slow cooker pot. Pour over the hot mushroom mixture and spread into an even layer. Cover and cook on Low for 2½–3 hours or until the pasta is just tender. Spoon into shallow bowls. Serve sprinkled with Parmesan cheese, if liked.

For mushroom pastichio, follow the recipe above, using 250 g (8 oz) macaroni instead of the rigatoni. Mix 3 eggs with 250 ml (8 fl oz) natural yogurt, 75 g (3 oz) grated feta cheese and a pinch of grated nutmeg. Spoon the mixture over the top of the mushroom and pasta mixture for the last hour of cooking until set. Place under a preheated hot grill to brown the top before serving. **Calories per serving 416**

tomato & squash curry

Calories per serving **308 (not including rice)**
Serves **4**
Preparation time **20 minutes**
Cooking time **5–6 hours**

25 g (1 oz) **butter**
1 **onion**, chopped
400 g (13 oz) peeled
   butternut squash, diced
2 **garlic cloves**, finely chopped
3.5 cm (1 ½ inch) piece of
   fresh root ginger, finely
   chopped
½–1 **mild red chilli**, deseeded
   and finely chopped
4 tablespoons **ready-made
   korma curry paste**
150 ml (¼ pint) **vegetable
   stock**
625 g (1 ¼ lb) **plum
   tomatoes**, halved
50 g (2 oz) **creamed coconut**,
   crumbled
salt and **pepper**
roughly chopped **fresh
   coriander**, to garnish

Preheat the slow cooker if necessary. Heat the butter in a large frying pan over a medium heat, add the onion and cook for 5 minutes until softened. Stir in the butternut squash, garlic, ginger and chilli, to taste, and cook for 2–3 minutes. Mix in the curry paste and cook for 1 minute, then stir in the stock and bring to the boil.

Transfer the mixture to the slow cooker pot, then arrange the tomatoes, cut sides up, in a single layer on top. Sprinkle with the coconut and season to taste. Cover and cook on Low for 5–6 hours or until the squash is tender and the tomatoes are soft but still holding their shape.

Spoon into bowls, sprinkle with roughly chopped coriander and serve with pilau rice, if liked.

For quick pilau rice, to serve as an accompaniment, rinse 175 g (6 oz) basmati rice under cold running water, then drain. Heat 10 g (3¾ oz) butter and 1 tablespoon sunflower oil in a large frying pan, add 1 chopped onion and cook until softened. Stir in 1 dried red chilli, 1 cinnamon stick, halved, 1 teaspoon cumin seeds, 1 bay leaf, 6 crushed cardamom pods, ½ teaspoon ground turmeric and a little salt. Add 475 ml (16 fl oz) boiling water, cover and simmer gently for 10 minutes. Take off the heat and leave to stand for 5–8 minutes without lifting the lid. Fluff up with a fork before serving. **Calories per serving 189**

eve's pudding

Calories per serving **335**
Serves **4**
Preparation time **25 minutes**
Cooking time **3–3½ hours**

50 g (2 oz) **sunflower margarine**, plus extra for greasing
50 g (2 oz) **caster sugar**
50 g (2 oz) **self-raising flour**
25 g (1 oz) **ground almonds**
¼ teaspoon **baking powder**
1 **egg**
grated rind and juice of 1 **lemon**
1 **dessert apple**, quartered, cored and sliced
1 tablespoon **apricot jam**
75 g (3 oz) **instant powdered custard with sweetener**, to serve

Preheat the slow cooker if necessary. Grease the base and sides of a 15 cm (6 inch) round ovenproof dish, about 6 cm (2½ inches) deep, with a little margarine. Place the margarine, sugar, flour, almonds and baking powder in a food processor, add the egg and lemon rind and blend until smooth. Spoon into the dish and spread level.

Toss the apple slices with the lemon juice, then overlap in a ring on top of the pudding mixture. Cover the dish with greased foil and put in the slow cooker pot. Pour boiling water into the slow cooker pot to come halfway up the sides of the dish, cover and cook on High for 3–3½ hours until a knife comes out cleanly when inserted into the centre.

Dot the top of the pudding with the apricot jam, then gently spread into an even layer. Place under a preheated hot grill for 3–4 minutes until the top is lightly caramelized. Make the custard with boiling water according to packet instructions and serve with the pudding.

For chocolate & pear pudding, follow the recipe above to make the pudding base, using 1 tablespoon cocoa powder instead of the lemon rind. Quarter, core and slice 1 small pear, toss with the lemon juice, then arrange over the pudding mixture. Cover and bake as above, then dust the top with a little sifted icing sugar before serving. **Calories per serving 265**

honeyed rice pudding

Calories per serving **366 (not including cream)**
Preparation time **10 minutes**
Cooking temperature **low**
Cooking time **2½–3 hours**
Serves **4**

butter, for greasing
750 ml (1¼ pints) **full-fat Jersey milk**
3 tablespoons set **honey**
125 g (4 oz) **risotto rice**

Preheat the slow cooker if necessary; see the manufacturer's instructions. Lightly butter the inside of the slow cooker pot. Pour the milk into a saucepan, add the honey and bring just to the boil, stirring until the honey has melted. Pour into the slow cooker pot, add the rice and stir gently.

Cover with the lid and cook on low for 2½–3 hours, stirring once during cooking, or until the pudding is thickened and the rice is soft. Stir again just before spooning into dishes. Top each bowl with 1 tablespoon of jam and thick cream, if liked.

For vanilla rice pudding, pour the milk into a saucepan, replace the honey with 3 tablespoons caster sugar and bring just to the boil. Slit a vanilla pod, scrape the black seeds out with a small knife and add to the milk with the pod. Pour into the greased slow cooker pot, add the rice and cook as above. Remove the vanilla pod before serving with thick cream. **Calories per serving 364 (not including cream)**

blueberry & passion fruit cheesecake

Calories per serving **327**
Serves **4**
Preparation time **25 minutes,
plus cooling and chilling**
Cooking time **2–2½ hours**

1 tablespoon **sunflower
margarine**, plus extra for
greasing
75 g (3 oz) **reduced-fat
digestive biscuits**, finely
crushed
300 g (10 oz) **extra-light soft
cheese**
175 ml (6 fl oz) **0% fat Greek
yogurt**
1 tablespoon **cornflour**
finely grated rind and juice of
½ **lime**
1 teaspoon **vanilla extract**
3 tablespoons **granular
sweetener**
3 tablespoons **caster sugar**
2 **eggs**
125 g (4 oz) **blueberries**
2 **passion fruits**, halved

Preheat the slow cooker if necessary. Grease the base
and sides of a 15 cm (6 inch) round ovenproof dish,
about 6 cm (2½ inches) deep, with a little margarine.
Line the base with nonstick baking paper.

Melt the margarine in a small saucepan and stir in the
crushed biscuits. Spoon into the dish and press down
firmly to make a thin, even layer. Place the cheese,
yogurt and cornflour in a mixing bowl and whisk until
smooth. Add the lime rind and juice, vanilla, sweetener,
sugar and eggs and whisk again until smooth.

Pour the mixture into the dish and smooth the surface.
Cover with greased foil and put in the slow cooker pot.
Pour boiling water into the slow cooker pot to come
halfway up the sides of the dish, cover and cook on
High for 2–2½ hours or until the cheesecake is set
but with a slight wobble in the centre. Remove from
the slow cooker and leave to cool, then chill in the
refrigerator for 3–4 hours or overnight.

Loosen the edge of the cheesecake with a knife, turn
out of the dish and peel away the lining paper. Place on a
serving plate, pile the blueberries on top, then scoop the
passion fruit seeds over them. Serve cut into wedges.

For summer berry cheesecake, follow the recipe
above to make the cheesecake, using the grated rind
and juice of ½ lemon instead of the lime. Gently toss
100 g (3½ oz) sliced strawberries and 100 g (3½ oz)
raspberries with 2 tablespoons reduced-sugar strawberry
jam and 1 tablespoon lemon juice instead of the blueberries
and passion fruits. Turn out the cheesecake and top
with the berry mixture just before serving. **Calories
per serving 345**

recipes
under 500
calories

balsamic beef hotpot

Calories per serving **408**
Serves **4**
Preparation time **30 minutes**
Cooking time **7¼–8¼ hours**

low-calorie cooking oil spray
600 g (1 lb) **lean stewing
 beef**, trimmed of fat and
 cubed
1 **onion**, chopped
250 g (8 oz) **swede**, cut into
 2 cm (¾ inch) cubes
300 g (10 oz) **carrots**, sliced
150 g (5 oz) **mushrooms**,
 sliced
2 teaspoons **plain flour**
450 ml (¾ pint) **beef stock**
2 tablespoons **balsamic
 vinegar**
1 teaspoon **mustard powder**
500 g (1 lb) **potatoes**, sliced
salt and **pepper**
1 tablespoon chopped
 parsley, to garnish

To serve
200 g (7 oz) **broccoli florets**,
 steamed
200 g (7 oz) **sugar snap
 peas**, steamed

Preheat the slow cooker if necessary. Spray a large frying pan with a little low-calorie cooking oil spray and place over a high heat until hot. Add the beef, a few pieces at a time until all the beef is in the pan, and cook for 5 minutes, stirring, until browned. Use a slotted spoon to transfer the beef to the slow cooker pot.

Add a little more low-calorie cooking oil spray to the pan, add the onion and cook for 4–5 minutes until beginning to brown. Add the swede, carrots and mushrooms and cook for 2 minutes. Add the flour and stir well.

Stir in the stock, vinegar and mustard, season to taste and bring to the boil. Pour over the beef in the slow cooker pot. Arrange the potato slices on top, slightly overlapping. Season lightly, then press the potatoes into the stock.

Cover and cook on High for 7–8 hours until the potatoes and beef are tender. Spray the potatoes with a little extra low-calorie cooking oil spray, then place the slow cooker pot under a preheated hot grill until the potatoes are golden. Sprinkle with the parsley and serve with the steamed vegetables.

For mustard beef hotpot, follow the recipe above, using 1 tablespoon wholegrain mustard in place of the balsamic vinegar and mustard powder. **Calories per serving 409**

spiced beef & red pepper stew

Calories per serving **469**
Serves **4**
Preparation time **20 minutes**
Cooking time **8–10 hours**

low-calorie cooking oil spray
500 g (1 lb) **stewing beef**,
  trimmed of fat and cubed
2 **red onions**, cut into wedges
2 **celery sticks**, thickly sliced
2 **red peppers**, cored,
  deseeded and cut into
  chunks
2 **garlic cloves**, finely chopped
1 teaspoon **cumin seeds**,
  roughly crushed
1 teaspoon **chilli powder**
2 teaspoons **plain flour**
450 ml (¾ pint) **beef stock**
1 tablespoon **tomato purée**
salt and **pepper**

To serve
4 tablespoons chopped **fresh
  coriander**
250 g (8 oz) **long-grain rice**,
  boiled

Preheat the slow cooker if necessary. Spray a large frying pan with a little low-calorie cooking oil spray and place over a high heat until hot. Add the beef, a few pieces at a time until all the beef is in the pan, and cook for 5 minutes, stirring, until browned. Use a slotted spoon to transfer the beef to the slow cooker pot.

Add a little more low-calorie cooking oil spray to the pan, add the onion wedges and cook for 2–3 minutes, stirring. Add the celery and red pepper, then stir in the garlic, cumin and chilli powder and cook for 1 minute.

Stir in the flour, then add the stock and tomato purée, season to taste and bring to the boil, stirring. Spoon over the beef, cover and cook on Low for 8–10 hours until the beef is tender.

Stir the chopped coriander into the cooked rice and spoon into shallow bowls. Stir the beef casserole, spoon over the rice and serve.

For Chinese gingered beef, follow the recipe above, replacing the cumin seeds and chilli powder with 2 tablespoons soy sauce and 2 tablespoons finely chopped fresh root ginger. Serve with 250 g (8 oz) Chinese egg noodles, cooked according to packet instructions. **Calories per serving 490**

pulled pork

Calories per serving **408**
Serves **4**
Preparation time **15 minutes**
Cooking time **5–6 hours**

700 g (1 lb 6 oz) boneless
  pork shoulder joint,
  trimmed of fat
1 tablespoon **treacle**
½ teaspoon **ground allspice**
½ teaspoon **ground ginger**
½ teaspoon **ground cumin**
½ teaspoon **dried chilli flakes**
¼ teaspoon **salt**
leaves from 2–3 **thyme sprigs**
1 **onion**, sliced
200 ml (7 fl oz) hot **chicken
  stock**
pepper

To serve
4 **hamburger buns**, split
4 **lettuce leaves**, shredded
3 **tomatoes**, thinly sliced
1 **dill cucumber**, drained and
  sliced

Preheat the slow cooker if necessary. Unroll the pork joint and make a cut through the middle to reduce the thickness by half. Place in the slow cooker pot and spread with the treacle.

Mix the ground spices, chilli flakes, salt and thyme leaves and season with pepper. Rub over the pork joint, then tuck the onion slices around it. Pour the hot stock over the onions, then cover and cook on High for 5–6 hours or until the pork is very tender.

Place the pork on a chopping board and pull into shreds using two forks. Top the bottom halves of the buns with the lettuce, tomato and dill cucumber, then pile the hot pork on top. Add a few of the onion slices to each bun and drizzle with the cooking juices. Replace the tops of the buns and serve immediately.

For herby pulled pork, follow the recipe above to prepare the pork and spread it with the treacle. Mix the chilli flakes, salt and thyme leaves with 2 finely chopped sage sprigs and rub over the treacle-spread pork. Add the onion and stock and continue as above. **Calories per serving 408**

warming lamb pot roast

Calories per serving **417**
Serves **4**
Preparation time **20 minutes**
Cooking time **5–6 hours**

low-calorie cooking oil spray
875 g (1¾ lb) **leg of lamb** on
   the bone
1 **leek**, thickly sliced
2 teaspoons **plain flour**
450 ml (¾ pint) **lamb stock**
1 tablespoon **redcurrant jelly**
15 g (½ oz) **mint leaves**,
   chopped, plus extra to
   garnish
200 g (7 oz) **celeriac**, cut into
   2 cm (¾ inch) cubes
200 g (7 oz) **swede**, cut into
   2 cm (¾ inch) cubes
300 g (10 oz) **baby**
   Chantenay carrots, halved
   lengthways
salt and **pepper**

Preheat the slow cooker if necessary. Spray a large frying pan with a little low-calorie cooking oil spray and place over a high heat until hot. Season the lamb and seal in the hot pan for 5–10 minutes, turning until browned on all sides. Transfer to the slow cooker pot.

Add the white leek slices (reserving the green slices) to the frying pan with a little extra low-calorie cooking oil spray, cook for 2–3 minutes, then sprinkle in the flour and stir well. Add the stock, redcurrant jelly and mint, then bring to the boil, stirring.

Arrange the celeriac, swede and carrots around the lamb, then pour over the leeks and stock. Cover and cook on High for 5–6 hours until the lamb starts to fall off the bone and the vegetables are tender, adding the reserved green leek slices for the last 15 minutes of cooking.

Serve the lamb in shallow bowls with the hot vegetables and stock, garnished with extra mint. If you prefer a thicker sauce, drain the stock into a small saucepan and boil rapidly to reduce by half.

For lamb pot roast with flageolet beans, follow the recipe above, adding a 400 g (13 oz) can of flageolet beans, drained, 2 rosemary sprigs and 2 finely chopped garlic cloves instead of the mint, swede and celeriac. **Calories per serving 459**

skinny spaghetti bolognese

Calories per serving **490**
Serves **4**
Preparation time **20 minutes**
Cooking time **8–10 hours**

low-calorie cooking oil spray
500 g (1 lb) **extra-lean minced beef**
1 **onion**, finely chopped
2 **garlic cloves**, finely chopped
1 **carrot**, coarsely grated
2 **courgettes**, coarsely grated
150 g (5 oz) **button mushrooms**, sliced
500 g (1 lb) **passata**
150 ml (¼ pint) **beef stock**
1 teaspoon **dried oregano**
salt and **pepper**

To serve
300 g (10 oz) **dried spaghetti**
handful of **oregano** or **basil leaves**

Spray a large frying pan with a little low-calorie cooking oil spray and place over a high heat until hot. Add the minced beef and onion and cook for 5 minutes, stirring and breaking up the mince with a wooden spoon until evenly browned.

Stir in the garlic, carrot, courgette and mushrooms. Add the passata, stock and oregano, then season to taste. Bring to the boil, stirring. Transfer to the slow cooker pot, cover and cook on Low for 8–10 hours.

Cook the spaghetti in a large saucepan of lightly salted boiling water according to packet instructions, until tender. Drain well, toss with the Bolognese sauce and serve immediately sprinkled with oregano or basil leaves.

For Italian shepherd's pie, make the Bolognese sauce as above. Peel 500 g (1 lb) potatoes and 500 g (1 lb) swede and cut into chunks. Cook in a saucepan of lightly salted boiling water for 15–20 minutes until tender. Drain and mash with 4 tablespoons vegetable stock (or 4 tablespoons cooking water). Beat 1 egg and stir half into the mash, then season to taste. Spoon the mash over the Bolognese sauce and rough up the top with a fork. Brush with the remaining beaten egg and brown under the grill before serving. **Calories per serving 258**

french-style chicken pot roast

Calories per serving **495**
Serves **4**
Preparation time **20 minutes**
Cooking time **5¼–6¼ hours**

1.35 kg (2 lb 10 oz) **oven-ready chicken**
225 g (7½ oz) **baby new potatoes**, halved
1 **red pepper**, cored, deseeded and diced
1 **yellow pepper**, cored, deseeded and diced
4 **garlic cloves**, halved
200 g (7 oz) **cherry tomatoes**, halved
½ **lemon**, sliced
small bunch of **basil**
300 ml (½ pint) hot **chicken stock**
1 tablespoon **tomato purée**
3 teaspoons **granular sweetener**
40 g (1½ oz) **pitted green olives** in brine, drained and halved
salt and **pepper**

Preheat the slow cooker if necessary. Put the chicken into the slow cooker pot, then tuck the potatoes, peppers, garlic and tomatoes around it. Season the chicken, then arrange the lemon slices over the breast. Tear half the basil into pieces and sprinkle over the chicken and vegetables.

Mix the hot stock with the tomato purée and sweetener, then pour into the slow cooker pot and add the olives. Cover and cook on High for 5–6 hours or until the chicken is thoroughly cooked and the meat juices run clear when the thickest parts of the leg and breast are pierced with a sharp knife.

Place the slow cooker pot under a preheated hot grill until the chicken is golden. Cut the meat off the bones and arrange it in shallow bowls with the vegetables and stock, garnished with the remaining basil. If you prefer a thicker sauce, drain the stock into a small saucepan and boil rapidly to reduce by half.

For lemon & tarragon pot-roasted chicken, place the chicken in the slow cooker pot and tuck 225 g (7½ oz) halved baby new potatoes, 3 chopped carrots, 3 chopped celery sticks and 2 tarragon sprigs around it. Season the chicken and cover the breast with ½ sliced lemon. Mix 300 ml (½ pint) hot chicken stock with 1 tablespoon tomato purée and 3 teaspoons Dijon mustard and pour over the chicken. Cook as above and serve garnished with extra tarragon. **Calories per serving 470**

tipsy mustard pork

Calories per serving **423**
Serves **4**
Preparation time **20 minutes**
Cooking time **4–5 hours**

low-calorie cooking oil spray
4 **pork loin chops** on the
  bone, 225 g (7½ oz) each,
  trimmed of fat
1 **onion**, chopped
1 tablespoon **plain flour**
2 teaspoons **wholegrain
  mustard**
1 teaspoon **ground turmeric**
150 ml (¼ pint) **dry cider**
300 ml (½ pint) **chicken stock**
500 g (1 lb) **swede**, cut into
  2.5 cm (1 inch) pieces
250 g (8 oz) **potatoes**, cut
  into 2.5 cm (1 inch) pieces
1 **dessert apple**, cored and
  thickly sliced
salt and **pepper**
200 g (7 oz) **sugar snap
  peas**, steamed, to serve

Preheat the slow cooker if necessary. Spray a large frying pan with a little low-calorie cooking oil spray and place over a high heat until hot. Add the chops in a single layer, cook for 5 minutes, turning once, until browned on both sides, then transfer to a plate.

Add a little extra low-calorie cooking oil spray to the pan if necessary, then add the onion and cook over a medium heat for 4–5 minutes until softened. Stir in the flour, then add the mustard, turmeric, cider and stock. Season to taste and bring to the boil, stirring.

Place the swede and potato in the slow cooker pot. Arrange the pork chops in a single layer on top, then add the apple slices. Pour over the hot stock mixture, cover and cook on High for 4–5 hours until the pork is very tender.

Transfer the pork to a plate. Divide the vegetables between 4 shallow dishes, top with the chops and drizzle with the sauce. Serve with steamed sugar snap peas.

For mustard chicken with celeriac, follow the recipe above, browning 4 skinless chicken leg joints in the frying pan instead of the pork chops. Continue, replacing the swede with 500 g (1 lb) diced celeriac. Cook on Low for 8–10 hours until the chicken is cooked through with no hint of pink juices and the celeriac is tender. **Calories per serving 413**

pork puttanesca

Calories per serving **403**
Serves **4**
Preparation time **20 minutes**
Cooking time **7–8 hours**

low-calorie cooking oil spray
625 g (1 ¼ lb) **lean pork**,
   diced
1 **onion**, chopped
2 **garlic cloves**, finely chopped
400 g (13 oz) can **chopped
   tomatoes**
4 teaspoons **sherry vinegar**
15 g (½ oz) **basil**, roughly torn,
   plus extra to garnish
1 tablespoon **capers** in brine,
   drained and chopped
50 g (2 oz) **pitted olives**,
   chopped
salt and **pepper**
chopped **parsley**, to garnish
175 g (6 oz) **spaghetti**, boiled

Preheat the slow cooker if necessary. Spray a large frying pan with a little low-calorie cooking oil spray and place over a high heat until hot. Add the pork, a few pieces at a time until all the pork is in the pan, and cook for 5 minutes, stirring, until browned. Use a slotted spoon to transfer the pork to a plate.

Add a little more low-calorie cooking oil spray to the frying pan if necessary, then add the onion and cook for 4–5 minutes, stirring, until just beginning to brown. Add the garlic, tomatoes, vinegar and basil and bring to the boil, stirring.

Mix the capers and olives together and add half to the sauce, reserving the rest for garnish.

Transfer the pork to the slow cooker pot, then pour over the sauce. Cover and cook on High for 7–8 hours until the pork is tender. Stir, then sprinkle with the reserved capers and olives, some extra basil and a little chopped parsley. Serve with the cooked spaghetti.

For pork osso bucco, follow the recipe above, using 2 tablespoons chopped parsley mixed with the grated rind of 1 lemon and 2 finely chopped garlic cloves instead of the capers and olives. Serve with 225 g (7½ oz) rice, boiled with a few strands of saffron.
Calories per serving 436

lamb steaks with cumberland sauce

Calories per serving **441**
Serves **4**
Preparation time **20 minutes**
Cooking time **8¼–10¼ hours**

1 tablespoon **sunflower oil**
800 g (1 lb 9 oz) **lamb rump steaks**, trimmed of fat
1 **onion**, sliced
2 teaspoons **plain flour**
125 ml (4 fl oz) **red wine**
125 ml (4 fl oz) **lamb stock**
finely shredded rind and juice of 1 **orange**
finely shredded rind and juice of 1 **lemon**
2.5 cm (1 inch) piece of **fresh root ginger**, finely chopped
1 tablespoon **tomato purée**
1 tablespoon **redcurrant jelly**
1 tablespoon **granular sweetener**
salt and **pepper**
750 g (1 ½lb) **celeriac**, diced, to serve

Preheat the slow cooker if necessary. Heat the oil in a large frying pan over a high heat until hot. Add the lamb and cook for 2–3 minutes, turning once, until browned on both sides. Use a slotted spoon to transfer the lamb to the slow cooker pot.

Add the onion to the pan and cook for 4–5 minutes over a medium heat, stirring until softened. Stir in the flour, then add the wine, stock, half the orange and lemon rind, the orange and lemon juice, the ginger, tomato purée, redcurrant jelly and sweetener. Season to taste and bring to the boil, stirring. Pour the mixture over the lamb, cover and cook on Low for 8–10 hours.

Cook the celeriac in a saucepan of lightly salted boiling water for 10–15 minutes until tender. Mash with a little of the cooking water until smooth and season to taste. Serve with the lamb in bowls, garnished with the remaining orange and lemon rind.

For lamb steaks with cranberry sauce, follow the recipe above, using 25 g (1 oz) dried cranberries and 1 tablespoon cranberry sauce instead of the ginger and redcurrant jelly. Cook and serve as above. **Calories per serving 444**

peasant paella

Calories per serving **499**
Serves **4**
Preparation time **20 minutes**
Cooking time **5–6¼ hours**

low-calorie cooking oil spray
500 g (1 lb) boneless, skinless
   chicken thighs, cubed
1 **onion**, chopped
60 g (2¼ oz) **chorizo**, sliced
2 **garlic cloves**, finely chopped
1 **red pepper**, cored,
   deseeded and diced
1 **orange pepper**, cored,
   deseeded and diced
2 **celery sticks**, diced
2 pinches of **saffron threads**
½ teaspoon **dried**
   Mediterranean herbs
750 ml (1¼ pints) hot **chicken**
   stock
175 g (6 oz) **long-grain**
   brown rice
125 g (4 oz) **frozen peas**
salt and **pepper**
2 tablespoons **chopped**
   parsley, to garnish

Preheat the slow cooker if necessary. Spray a large frying pan with a little low-calorie cooking oil spray and place over a high heat until hot. Add the chicken, a few pieces at a time until all the chicken is in the pan, and cook for 5 minutes, stirring, until browned. Use a slotted spoon to transfer the chicken to the slow cooker pot.

Add the onion, chorizo and garlic to the frying pan and cook for 3–4 minutes, stirring until the onion is beginning to colour. Add the peppers and celery, stir well, then transfer to the slow cooker pot. Mix the saffron and dried herbs with the hot stock, season to taste, then pour into the slow cooker pot and stir well. Cover and cook on High for 3–4 hours.

Place the rice in a sieve and rinse under cold running water, then stir into the chicken mixture. Cover again and cook for 1½–1¾ hours until the rice is tender. Stir in the peas and continue cooking for 15 minutes. Serve garnished with chopped parsley.

For seafood paella, follow the recipe above to cook the paella, omitting the chicken. Defrost a 400 g (13 oz) packet of frozen mixed seafood and pat dry on kitchen paper. Spray a large frying pan with a little low-calorie cooking oil spray and place over a high heat until hot. Add the seafood and fry for 4–5 minutes until piping hot. Stir into the finished paella and garnish with the parsley. **Calories per serving 385**

chicken cacciatore

Calories per serving **453**
Serves **4**
Preparation time **20 minutes**
Cooking time **8–9 hours**

low-calorie cooking oil spray
500 g (1 lb) boneless, skinless
  chicken thighs, cubed
1 **onion**, chopped
2 **garlic cloves**, finely chopped
1 **red pepper**, cored,
  deseeded and diced
1 **orange pepper**, cored,
  deseeded and diced
2 **celery sticks**, diced
150 ml (¼ pint) **chicken stock**
400 g (13 oz) can **chopped
  tomatoes**
1 tablespoon **tomato purée**
1 tablespoon **balsamic
  vinegar**
leaves from 2 **rosemary
  sprigs**, chopped
salt and **pepper**
2 tablespoons chopped
  parsley, to garnish
200 g (7 oz) **dried tagliatelle**,
  to serve

Preheat the slow cooker if necessary. Spray a large frying pan with a little low-calorie cooking oil spray and place over a high heat until hot. Add the chicken, a few pieces at a time until all the chicken is in the pan, and cook for 3–4 minutes, stirring, until just beginning to brown. Add the onion and continue to cook until the chicken is golden and the onion has softened.

Stir in the garlic, peppers and celery, then add the stock, tomatoes, tomato purée, balsamic vinegar and rosemary. Season generously and bring to the boil, stirring. Transfer to the slow cooker pot, cover and cook on Low for 8–9 hours until the chicken is tender and cooked through.

Meanwhile, cook the tagliatelle in a saucepan of lightly salted boiling water according to packet instructions until tender. Drain, then toss with the chicken mixture and serve garnished with parsley.

For potato-topped cacciatore, follow the recipe above and place all the ingredients in the slow cooker pot. Thinly slice 625 g (1 ¼ lb) potatoes and arrange them on top of the chicken mixture, overlapping. Press the potatoes down into the liquid, then cover and cook on High for 5–6 hours until the potatoes and chicken are cooked through. Spray the potatoes with a little extra low-calorie cooking oil spray, then place the slow cooker pot under a hot grill until the potatoes are golden, if liked. **Calories per serving 403**

spicy turkey tortillas

Calories per serving **468**
Serves **4**
Preparation time **20 minutes**
Cooking time **8¼–10¼ hours**

low-calorie cooking oil spray
400 g (13 oz) **minced turkey breast**
1 **onion**, chopped
2 **garlic cloves**, finely chopped
1 teaspoon **dried chilli flakes**
1 teaspoon **cumin seeds**, crushed
1 teaspoon **mild paprika**
400 g (13 oz) can **chopped tomatoes**
200 g (7 oz) can **red kidney beans**, drained
150 ml (¼ pint) **chicken stock**
1 tablespoon **tomato purée**
1 **red pepper**, cored, deseeded and diced

To serve
4 x 20 cm (8 inch) **soft tortilla wraps**, 40 g (1½ oz) each
50 g (2 oz) **salad leaves**
4 tablespoons **0% fat Greek yogurt**
40 g (1½ oz) **reduced-fat Cheddar cheese**, grated
fresh coriander, torn

Preheat the slow cooker if necessary. Spray a large frying pan with a little low-calorie cooking oil spray and place over a high heat until hot. Add the minced turkey and onion and fry for 4–5 minutes, stirring and breaking up the mince with a wooden spoon until it is just beginning to brown.

Stir in the garlic, chilli, cumin seeds and paprika, then add the tomatoes, kidney beans, stock and tomato purée. Add the red pepper, season to taste and bring to the boil. Transfer to the slow cooker pot, cover and cook on Low for 8–10 hours until the turkey is cooked through.

Warm the tortillas in a hot dry frying pan for 1–2 minutes each side, then place on 4 serving plates. Spoon the spicy turkey on top, then add a handful of salad leaves to each, a spoonful of yogurt, a little Cheddar and some torn coriander. Serve immediately.

For spicy turkey thatch, follow the recipe above to make and cook the spicy turkey mixture. Cook, drain and mash 750 g (1½ lb) potatoes, stir in 4 tablespoons vegetable stock and season to taste. Place the turkey mixture in a shallow heatproof dish and spoon the mashed potato on top. Rough up the top with a fork, then brush with ½ beaten egg. Brown under the grill before serving. **Calories per serving 440**

sticky jerk ribs

Calories per serving **435**
Serves **4**
Preparation time **20 minutes**
Cooking time **5¼–6¼ hours**

1.25 kg (2½ lb) **lean pork ribs**
1 **onion**, cut into wedges
1 large **carrot**, sliced
3 **bay leaves**
2 tablespoons **malt vinegar**
low-calorie cooking oil spray
salt and **pepper**

Jerk glaze
8 tablespoons **passata**
3 tablespoons **soy sauce**
½ teaspoon **ground cinnamon**
½ teaspoon **ground allspice**
¼ teaspoon **chilli powder**
1 tablespoon **dark muscovado sugar**
grated rind and juice of ½ **orange**
4 **spring onions**, finely chopped

Preheat the slow cooker if necessary. Place the pork ribs, onion and carrot in the slow cooker pot and add the bay leaves and vinegar. Season generously, then pour over enough boiling water to cover the ribs, making sure the level is at least 2.5 cm (1 inch) from the top of the pot. Cover and cook on High for 5–6 hours until the meat is starting to fall away from the bones. Transfer the ribs to a foil-lined grill pan or baking sheet.

Mix together the glaze ingredients, then brush all over the ribs. Spray with a little low-calorie cooking oil spray and cook under a preheated hot grill, with the ribs about 5 cm (2 inches) away from the heat, for about 10 minutes, turning from time to time and brushing with the pan juices until a deep brown. Serve with salad, if liked.

For sticky hoisin ribs, follow the recipe above to cook the ribs in the slow cooker. Make a glaze by mixing together 3 tablespoons hoisin sauce, 8 tablespoons passata, ¼ teaspoon chilli powder, grated rind and juice of ½ orange and 4 finely chopped spring onions. Brush over the ribs and grill as above. **Calories per serving 436**

turkey kheema mutter

Calories per serving **454**
Serves **4**
Preparation time **15 minutes**
Cooking time **8½–10½ hours**

low-calorie cooking oil spray
500 g (1 lb) **minced turkey breast**
1 **onion**, chopped
2 **garlic cloves**, finely chopped
2.5 cm (1 inch) piece of **fresh root ginger**, finely chopped
1 teaspoon **cumin seeds**, crushed
4 teaspoons **medium-hot curry powder**
500 g (1 lb) **passata**
2 teaspoons **granular sweetener**
150 g (5 oz) **frozen peas**
4 tablespoons chopped **fresh coriander**
salt and **pepper**
½ **red onion**, thinly sliced, to garnish
4 small **chapatis**, 50 g (2 oz) each, to serve

Preheat the slow cooker if necessary. Spray a large frying pan with a little low-calorie cooking oil spray and place over a high heat until hot. Add the minced turkey and onion and fry for 4–5 minutes, stirring and breaking up the mince with a wooden spoon until it is just beginning to brown.

Stir in the garlic, ginger, cumin and curry powder and cook for 1 minute, then add the passata and sweetener. Season to taste and bring to the boil, stirring. Transfer to the slow cooker pot, cover and cook on Low for 8–10 hours until the turkey is cooked through.

Add the frozen peas to the slow cooker pot with half the coriander. Cover again and cook on High for 15 minutes. Sprinkle with the remaining coriander and the red onion and serve with the chapatis.

For kheema mutter jackets, follow the recipe above to make and cook the turkey and pea mixture. Scrub and prick 4 baking potatoes, 175 g (6 oz) each, place in the microwave on a sheet of kitchen paper and cook on full power for about 20 minutes, until tender. Transfer to serving plates, cut in half and top with the kheema mutter, remaining coriander and sliced red onion.
Calories per serving 399

sweet & sour chicken

Calories per serving **459**
Serves **4**
Preparation time **20 minutes**
Cooking time **6½–8½ hours**

1 tablespoon **sunflower oil**
1 kg (2 lb) boneless, skinless **chicken thighs**, cubed
4 **spring onions**, thickly sliced
2 **carrots**, halved lengthways and thinly sliced
2.5 cm (1 inch) piece of **fresh root ginger**, finely chopped
425 g (14 oz) can **pineapple chunks** in natural juice
300 ml (½ pint) **chicken stock**
1 tablespoon **cornflour**
1 tablespoon **tomato purée**
2 tablespoons **caster sugar**
2 tablespoons **soy sauce**
2 tablespoons **malt vinegar**
225 g (7½ oz) can **bamboo shoots**, drained
125 g (4 oz) **bean sprouts**
100 g (3½ oz) **mangetout**, thinly sliced
150 g (5 oz) **rice**, boiled

Preheat the slow cooker if necessary. Heat the oil in a large frying pan over a high heat, add the chicken and cook for 3–4 minutes until browned on all sides. Add the white spring onion slices (reserving the green slices), the carrots and ginger and cook for 2 minutes.

Stir in the pineapple chunks and their juice and the stock. Put the cornflour, tomato purée and sugar in a small bowl, then mix in the soy sauce and vinegar to make a smooth paste. Add to the pan and bring to the boil, stirring.

Transfer the chicken mixture to the slow cooker pot, add the bamboo shoots and press the chicken pieces into the liquid. Cover and cook on Low for 6–8 hours until the chicken is cooked through.

Add the reserved green spring onion slices, the bean sprouts and mangetout and mix well. Cover again and cook for 15 minutes or until the vegetables are just tender. Serve with the boiled rice.

For lemon chicken, follow the recipe above as far as the addition of the chicken stock. Mix the cornflour to a smooth paste with the juice of 1 lemon, then stir into the pan with 2 tablespoons dry sherry and 4 teaspoons caster sugar. Bring to the boil, stirring, then transfer to the slow cooker pot and cook as above, adding the green spring onion slices, bean sprouts and mangetout at the end. **Calories per serving 438**

beery barley beef

Calories per serving **439**
Serves **4**
Preparation time **15 minutes**
Cooking time **9–10 hours**

1 tablespoon **sunflower oil**
625 g (1¼ lb) **lean stewing
  beef**, cubed
1 **onion**, chopped
1 tablespoon **plain flour**
250 g (8 oz) **carrots**, diced
250 g (8 oz) **parsnips** or
  potatoes, diced
300 ml (½ pint) **light ale**
750 ml (1¼ pint) **beef stock**
small bunch of **mixed herbs** or
  dried bouquet garni
100 g (3½ oz) **pearl barley**
salt and **pepper**

Preheat the slow cooker if necessary. Heat the oil in a frying pan, add the beef a few pieces at a time until it is all in the pan, then fry over a high heat, stirring, until browned. Remove the beef with a slotted spoon and transfer to the slow cooker pot.

Add the onion to the frying pan and fry, stirring, for 5 minutes or until lightly browned. Mix in the flour, then add the root vegetables and beer and bring to the boil, stirring. Pour into the slow cooker pot.

Add the stock to the frying pan with the herbs and a little salt and pepper, bring to the boil, then pour into the slow cooker pot. Add the pearl barley, cover with the lid and cook on low for 9–10 hours until the beef is tender. Serve with herb croutons, if liked.

For herb croutons to accompany the beef, beat 2 tablespoons chopped parsley, 2 tablespoons chopped chives and 1 tablespoon chopped tarragon and a little black pepper into 75 g (3 oz) soft butter. Thickly slice ½ French stick, toast lightly on both sides, then spread with the herb butter. **Calories per serving 433**

tuna arrabiata

Calories per serving **481**
Serves **4**
Preparation time **20 minutes**
Cooking time **4–5 hours**

1 tablespoon **olive oil**
1 **onion**, chopped
2 **garlic cloves**, finely chopped
1 **red pepper**, cored,
   deseeded and diced
1 teaspoon **smoked paprika**
¼–½ teaspoon **dried chilli
   flakes**
400 g (13 oz) can **chopped
   tomatoes**
150 ml (¼ pint) **vegetable** or
   fish stock
200 g (7 oz) can **tuna** in water,
   drained
salt and **pepper**

To serve
375 g (12 oz) **dried spaghetti**
4 tablespoons grated
   Parmesan cheese
small handful of **basil leaves**

Preheat the slow cooker if necessary. Heat the oil in a large frying pan over a medium heat, add the onion and cook, stirring, for 5 minutes or until just browning around the edges. Add the garlic, red pepper, paprika and dried chillies and cook for 2 minutes.

Add the tomatoes and stock and season to taste. Bring to the boil, then transfer to the slow cooker pot. Break the tuna into large pieces and stir into the tomato mixture. Cover and cook on Low for 4–5 hours.

Meanwhile, cook the spaghetti in a saucepan of lightly salted boiling water according to packet instructions until tender. Drain and stir into the tomato sauce. Spoon into shallow bowls and sprinkle with the grated Parmesan and basil leaves.

For double tomato arrabiata, follow the recipe above using 75 g (3 oz) sliced sun-dried tomatoes and 100 g (3½ oz) sliced button mushrooms instead of the tuna. Cook and serve as above. **Calories per serving 479**

smoked mackerel kedgeree

Calories per serving **492**
Serves **4**
Preparation time **15 minutes**
Cooking time **3½–4½ hours**

1 tablespoon **sunflower oil**
1 **onion**, chopped
1 teaspoon **ground turmeric**
2 tablespoons **mango chutney**
about 750 ml (1¼ pints) **vegetable stock**
1 **bay leaf**
150 g (5 oz) **easy-cook brown rice**
200 g (7 oz) **smoked mackerel fillets**, skinned
100 g (3½ oz) **frozen peas**
25 g (1 oz) **watercress** or **rocket leaves**
4 **hard-boiled eggs**, cut into wedges
salt and **pepper**

Preheat the slow cooker if necessary. Heat the oil in a large frying pan over a medium heat, add the onion and cook, stirring, for 5 minutes until softened. Add the turmeric, chutney, stock and bay leaf, season to taste and bring to the boil.

Pour into the slow cooker pot and add the rice. Arrange the smoked mackerel in the pot in a single layer, cover and cook on Low for 3–4 hours until the rice is tender and has absorbed almost all the stock.

Stir in the peas, breaking up the fish into chunky pieces. Add a little extra hot stock if the rice is very dry, cover again and cook for 15 minutes. Stir in the watercress or rocket, spoon on to plates and top with the egg wedges.

For smoked haddock kedgeree with cardamom, follow the recipe above, increasing the amount of rice to 175 g (6 oz) and using 4 crushed cardamom pods with their black seeds instead of the chutney. Replace the smoked mackerel with 400 g (13 oz) skinned smoked haddock fillet, cut into 2 pieces. Continue as above, omitting the rocket or watercress. Drizzle with 4 tablespoons double cream before serving. **Calories per serving 418**

new orleans chicken gumbo

Calories per serving **414 (not including rice)**
Serves **4**
Preparation time **20 minutes**
Cooking time **8½–10½ hours**

2 tablespoons **olive oil**
500 g (1 lb) boneless, skinless **chicken thighs**, cubed
75 g (3 oz) **chorizo**, diced
75 g (3 oz) **smoked bacon**, trimmed of fat and diced
1 **onion**, sliced
2 **garlic cloves**, chopped
2 tablespoons **plain flour**
600 ml (1 pint) **chicken stock**
2 **bay leaves**
2 **thyme sprigs**
¼–½ teaspoon **cayenne pepper**
3 **celery sticks**, sliced
½ each of 3 different coloured **peppers**, cored, deseeded and sliced
125 g (4 oz) **okra**, thickly sliced (optional)
salt
chopped **parsley**, to garnish

Preheat the slow cooker if necessary. Heat the oil in a large frying pan over a high heat, add the chicken a few pieces at time until all the chicken is in the pan, then add the chorizo and bacon and cook for 5 minutes, stirring, until the chicken is golden. Transfer to the slow cooker pot with a slotted spoon.

Add the onion to the frying pan and cook over a medium heat until softened. Mix in the garlic, then stir in the flour. Gradually add the stock, stirring, then add the herbs and cayenne, to taste, and season generously. Bring to the boil, stirring.

Add the celery and peppers to the slow cooker pot, then pour over the hot onion mixture. Cover and cook, on Low for 8–10 hours or until the chicken is cooked through.

Stir in the okra, if using, cover again and cook on High for 15 minutes or until the okra has just softened. Stir once more, then sprinkle with chopped parsley. Serve with rice, if liked.

For prawn gumbo soup, follow the recipe above omitting the chicken and replacing the chicken stock with 600 ml (1 pint) fish stock, and adding 2 sliced carrots, 2 diced sweet potatoes and 1 diced courgette to the slow cooker pot with the celery and peppers. Add 200 g (7 oz) large cooked peeled prawns to the pot with the okra, if using, and cook on High for 20–30 minutes or until the prawns are piping hot. Serve with rice, if liked. **Calories per serving 433**

turkey tagine

Calories per serving **401** (not
  including **couscous**)
Serves **4**
Preparation time **25 minutes**
Cooking time **6¼–7¼ hours**

1 **turkey drumstick**, 700 g
  (1 lb 6 oz)
1 tablespoon **olive oil**
1 **onion**, chopped
2 **garlic cloves**, finely chopped
2.5 cm (1 inch) piece of **fresh
  root ginger**, finely chopped
2 tablespoons **plain flour**
1 teaspoon **ground turmeric**
1 teaspoon **ground cinnamon**
1 teaspoon **ground coriander**
½ teaspoon **cumin seeds**
600 ml (1 pint) hot **chicken
  stock**
400 g (13 oz) can **chickpeas**,
  drained
200 g (7 oz) **parsnips**, diced
200 g (7 oz) **carrots**, diced
small bunch of **fresh
  coriander**, roughly chopped
salt and **pepper**

Check that the turkey drumstick will fit into the slow cooker pot before you begin, cutting off the knuckle end if necessary with a large knife, after hitting it with a rolling pin or hammer. Preheat the slow cooker if necessary.

Heat the oil in a frying pan over a high heat, add the drumstick and cook, turning, until golden-brown all over. Transfer to the slow cooker pot. Add the onion to the pan and cook over a medium heat for 5 minutes until softened. Stir in the garlic, ginger and flour, then mix in the spices. Gradually stir in the stock, season to taste and bring to the boil.

Pour the onion mixture over the turkey. Add the chickpeas and vegetables to the pot and press into the liquid. Cover and cook on High for 6–7 hours or until the meat is tender and almost falling off the bone.

Take the turkey meat off the bone, discarding the skin and tendons. Cut it into bite-sized pieces and return them to the slow cooker pot. Stir in the chopped coriander and serve with couscous, if liked.

For chillied chicken tagine, follow the recipe above, using 4 skinless chicken thigh and drumstick joints instead of the turkey and adding ½ teaspoon smoked hot paprika with the other spices. Cook on High for 5–6 hours. **Calories 401**

pot-roasted chicken with lemon

Calories per serving **481**
Serves **4**
Preparation time **25 minutes**
Cooking time **5–6 hours**

2 tablespoons **olive oil**
1.5 kg (3 lb) **oven-ready chicken**
1 large **onion**, cut into 6 wedges
500 ml (17 fl oz) **dry cider**
3 teaspoons **Dijon mustard**
2 teaspoons **caster sugar**
900 ml (1½ pints) hot **chicken stock**
3 **carrots**, cut into chunks
3 **celery sticks**, thickly sliced
1 **lemon**, cut into 6 wedges
6 **tarragon sprigs**
3 tablespoons **crème fraîche**
salt and **pepper**

Preheat the slow cooker if necessary. Heat the oil in a large frying pan over a high heat, add the chicken and cook for 10 minutes, turning occasionally, until browned all over. Transfer to the slow cooker pot, breast side down.

Add the onion wedges to the pan and cook over a medium heat for 3–4 minutes until lightly browned. Add the cider, mustard and sugar and season to taste. Bring to the boil, stirring, then pour over the chicken.

Add the hot stock, then the vegetables, lemon wedges and 3 sprigs of the tarragon, pressing the chicken and vegetables down into the liquid. Cover and cook on High for 5–6 hours or until the chicken is thoroughly cooked and the meat juices run clear when the thickest parts of the leg and breast are pierced with a sharp knife.

Transfer the chicken to a large serving plate and arrange the vegetables around it. Transfer 600 ml (1 pint) of the hot cooking stock to a jug. Reserve a sprig of tarragon to garnish, then chop the remainder and whisk into the jug with the crème fraîche to make a gravy. Adjust the seasoning to taste. Serve the chicken and vegetables garnished with the remaining tarragon.

For herby pot-roasted chicken, follow the recipe above, omitting the lemon and tarragon, and adding 25 g (1 oz) mixed herb sprigs, such as rosemary, sage or tarragon, and parsley or chives, to the slow cooker pot with the vegetables. Remove the herb sprigs before serving, and garnish the chicken with 3 tablespoons chopped parsley or chives. **Calories per serving 480**

fragrant spiced chicken

Calories per serving **490**
Serves **4**
Preparation time **15 minutes**
Cooking time **5¼–6¼ hours**

1.5 kg (3 lb) **oven-ready chicken**
1 **onion**, chopped
200 g (7 oz) **carrots**, sliced
7.5 cm (3 inch) piece of **fresh root ginger**, sliced
2 **garlic cloves**, sliced
1 large **mild red chilli**, halved
3 large **star anise**
4 tablespoons **soy sauce**
4 tablespoons **rice vinegar**
1 tablespoon **light muscovado sugar**
900 ml (1½ pints) boiling **water**
small bunch of **fresh coriander**
75 g (3 oz) **mangetout**, thickly sliced
150 g (5 oz) **pak choi**, thickly sliced
salt and **pepper**
200 g (7 oz) **dried egg noodles**, to serve

Preheat the slow cooker if necessary. Place chicken, breast side down, in the slow cooker pot. Add the onion, carrots, ginger, garlic, chilli and star anise and spoon over the soy sauce, vinegar and sugar. Pour over the boiling water.

Add the coriander stems, reserving the leaves, and season to taste. Cover cook on High for 5–6 hours or until the chicken is thoroughly cooked and the meat juices run clear when the thickest parts of the leg and breast are pierced with a sharp knife.

Transfer the chicken to a chopping board and keep warm. Add the mangetout and pak choi to the pot, cover again and cook for 5–10 minutes or until just wilted. Meanwhile, cook the noodles in a saucepan of lightly salted boiling water according to packet instructions, drain well and divide between 4 bowls.

Carve the chicken into bite-sized pieces and arrange on top of the noodles with the reserved coriander leaves, then ladle over the hot broth and serve immediately.

For Italian spiced chicken with pesto, put the chicken into the pot with 1 chopped onion, 200 g (7 oz) sliced carrots, 2 sliced garlic cloves, 1 sliced fennel bulb and 1 sliced lemon. Pour over the boiling water as above and replace the coriander with a small bunch of basil. Use 3 chopped tomatoes, 150 g (5 oz) chopped purple sprouting broccoli and 2 tablespoons pesto sauce instead of the mangetout and pak choi. Cook 250 g (8 oz) fresh tagliatelle according to packet instructions to serve with the chicken. **Calories per serving 454**

sweet potato & egg curry

Calories per serving **451 (not including rice)**
Serves **4**
Preparation time **15 minutes**
Cooking time **6½–8½ hours**

1 tablespoon **sunflower oil**
1 **onion**, chopped
1 teaspoon **cumin seeds**, roughly crushed
1 teaspoon **ground coriander**
1 teaspoon **ground turmeric**
1 teaspoon **garam masala**
½ teaspoon **dried chilli flakes**
300 g (10 oz) **sweet potatoes**, diced
2 **garlic cloves**, finely chopped
400 g (13 oz) can **chopped tomatoes**
400 g (13 oz) can **lentils**, drained
300 ml (½ pint) **vegetable stock**
1 teaspoon **caster sugar**
6 **hard-boiled eggs**, halved
150 g (5 oz) **frozen peas**
150 ml (¼ pint) **single cream**
small bunch of **fresh coriander**, torn
salt and **pepper**

Preheat the slow cooker if necessary. Heat the oil in a frying pan over a medium heat, add the onion and cook for 5 minutes until softened. Stir in the spices, sweet potatoes and garlic and cook for 2 minutes, stirring.

Add the tomatoes, lentils, stock and sugar and season to taste. Bring to the boil, stirring, then transfer to the slow cooker pot, cover and cook on Low for 6–8 hours until the sweet potatoes are tender.

Add the eggs to the slow cooker pot with the peas, cream and half the coriander. Cover again and cook for 15 minutes more. Serve in bowls, garnished with the remaining coriander.

For mixed vegetable curry, follow the recipe above, using 100 g (3½ oz) halved fine beans and 50 g (2 oz) shredded kale instead of the eggs, adding them to the slow cooker pot at the same time as the peas. **Calories per serving 335**

spiced date & chickpea pilaf

Calories per serving **442**
Serves **4**
Preparation time **15 minutes**
Cooking time **3–4 hours**

1 tablespoon **olive oil**
1 **onion**, chopped
1–2 **garlic cloves**, finely
  chopped
4 cm (1½ inch) piece of **fresh
  root ginger**, finely chopped
1 teaspoon **ground turmeric**
1 teaspoon **ground cumin**,
  plus extra to garnish
1 teaspoon **ground coriander**
200 g (7 oz) **easy-cook
  brown rice**, boiled
400 g (13 oz) can **chickpeas**,
  drained
75 g (3 oz) **pitted dates**,
  chopped
1 litre (1¾ pints) **vegetable
  stock**
salt and **pepper**

To serve
1 tablespoon **olive oil**
1 **onion**, thinly sliced
150 ml (¼ pint) **0% fat Greek
  yogurt**
small handful of chopped **fresh
  coriander**

Preheat the slow cooker if necessary. Heat the oil in
a large frying pan over a medium heat, add the onion
and cook for 5 minutes until softened. Stir in the garlic,
ginger and ground spices and cook for 1 minute.

Add the rice, chickpeas, dates and stock, season to
taste and bring to the boil, stirring. Pour into the slow
cooker pot, cover and cook on Low for 3–4 hours
until the rice is tender and nearly all the stock has
been absorbed.

Meanwhile, heat the remaining oil in a frying pan over
a medium heat, add the sliced onion and cook, stirring,
until crisp and golden.

Stir the pilaf, spoon into bowls and top each portion
with a spoonful of yogurt, a little extra cumin, some
crispy onions and a little chopped coriander.

For chicken & almond pilaf, follow the recipe above,
adding 450 g (14½ oz) diced boneless, skinless
chicken thighs to the frying pan with the chopped onion.
Continue as above, omitting the dates. To serve, top with
25 g (1 oz) toasted flaked almonds and a little chopped
mint instead of the crispy onions and coriander.
Calories per serving **489**

tarka dahl

Calories per serving **490**
Serves **4**
Preparation time **15 minutes**
Cooking time **3–4 hours**

250 g (8 oz) **dried red lentils**
1 **onion**, finely chopped
½ teaspoon **ground turmeric**
½ teaspoon **cumin seeds**,
  roughly crushed
2 cm (¾ inch) piece of **fresh
  root ginger**, finely chopped
200 g (7 oz) can **chopped
  tomatoes**
600 ml (1 pint) hot **vegetable
  stock**
salt and **pepper**
fresh coriander leaves, torn,
  to garnish

Tarka
1 tablespoon **sunflower oil**
2 teaspoons **black mustard
  seeds**
½ teaspoon **cumin seeds**,
  roughly crushed
pinch of **ground turmeric**
2 **garlic cloves**, finely chopped

To serve
150 ml (¼ pint) **natural yogurt**
2 warm **naan breads**, halved

Preheat the slow cooker if necessary. Place the lentils in a sieve, rinse under cold running water, drain, then place in the slow cooker pot with the onion, spices, ginger, tomatoes and hot stock. Season lightly, cover and cook on High for 3–4 hours or until the lentils are soft and tender.

Meanwhile, heat the oil for the tarka in a small frying pan, add the remaining tarka ingredients and cook, stirring, for 2 minutes.

Roughly mash the lentil mixture, then spoon into bowls. Top with spoonfuls of yogurt and drizzle with the tarka. Sprinkle with the coriander leaves and serve with warm naan bread, if liked. (Calories per serving without naan 285.)

For tarka dahl with spinach, follow the recipe above to cook the lentils, adding 125 g (4 oz) washed and roughly shredded spinach leaves for the last 15 minutes of cooking. Fry the tarka spices as above, adding ¼ teaspoon crushed dried red chilli seeds, if liked. **Calories per serving 295 (not including naan)**

oatmeal & mixed seed granola

Calories per serving **459**
Serves **4**
Preparation time **15 minutes**
Cooking time **2½–3 hours**

125 g (4 oz) **medium oatmeal**
50 g (2 oz) **jumbo porridge oats**
25 g (1 oz) **pumpkin seeds**
25 g (1 oz) **sunflower seeds**
15 g (½ oz) **golden linseeds**
¼ teaspoon **ground cinnamon**
1 tablespoon **olive oil**
3 tablespoons **date syrup**
juice of ½ **orange**
25 g (1 oz) **dried goji berries**

To serve
600 ml (1 pint) **skimmed milk**
sliced **banana**
sliced **strawberries**
raspberries

Preheat the slow cooker if necessary. Place the oatmeal, porridge oats and seeds in the slow cooker pot and stir well. Add the cinnamon, olive oil, date syrup and orange juice and mix again until thoroughly combined. Cover and cook on High for 1½–2 hours, stirring once or twice with a fork to break the mixture into clumps.

Remove the lid and cook for 1 hour more until the granola is crisp. Break up once more with a fork, add the goji berries, then leave to cool. Store in an airtight jar in the refrigerator until ready to serve.

Serve in bowls, topped with skimmed milk and the fruit.

For honeyed oatmeal & fruit granola, follow the recipe above, omitting the pumpkin seeds and using 3 tablespoons runny honey instead of the date syrup. Add 25 g (1 oz) dried cranberries and 25 g (1 oz) dried cherries instead of the goji berries and serve as above. Calories per serving 431

pineapple upside-down puddings

Calories per serving **410**
Serves **4**
Preparation time **20 minutes**
Cooking time **2–2½ hours**

4 tablespoons **golden syrup**
2 tablespoons **light muscovado sugar**
220 g (7½ oz) can **pineapple chunks**, drained
40 g (1½ oz) **glacé cherries**, roughly chopped
50 g (2 oz) **sunflower margarine**, plus extra for greasing
50 g (2 oz) **caster sugar**
50 g (2 oz) **self-raising flour**
25 g (1 oz) **desiccated coconut**
1 **egg**
1 tablespoon **milk**

Preheat the slow cooker if necessary. Lightly grease 4 metal pudding basins, 250 ml (8 fl oz) each, and line the bases with nonstick baking paper. Divide the golden syrup and muscovado sugar between them, then place three-quarters of the pineapple on top with the cherries.

Place the remaining pineapple with all the remaining ingredients into a mixing bowl and beat together until smooth. Spoon the mixture into the pudding basins, level the surfaces with the back of a small spoon, then cover the tops with greased foil and put in the slow cooker pot.

Pour boiling water into the slow cooker pot to come halfway up the sides of the basins, cover and cook on High for 2–2½ hours until the sponge is well risen and springs back when pressed with a fingertip.

Remove the foil, loosen the edges of the puddings with a round-bladed knife and turn out into shallow bowls. Peel away the lining paper and serve.

For plum & almond puddings, follow the recipe above, using 4 stoned and sliced red plums instead of the pineapple and cherries. Omit the coconut and add 25 g (1 oz) ground almonds and a few drops of almond essence to the sponge mixture instead. **Calories per serving 393**

gingered date & syrup puddings

Calories per serving **472**
Serves **4**
Preparation time **20 minutes**
Cooking time **3½–4 hours**

125 g (4 oz) **pitted dates**,
   chopped
125 ml (4 fl oz) boiling **water**
¼ teaspoon **bicarbonate of
   soda**
50 g (2 oz) **sunflower
   margarine**, plus extra for
   greasing
4 tablespoons **golden syrup**
50 g (2 oz) **light muscovado
   sugar**
100 g (3½ oz) **self-raising
   flour**
1 **egg**
1 teaspoon **vanilla extract**
1 teaspoon **ground ginger**
2 small scoops of **low-fat
   vanilla ice cream**

Preheat the slow cooker if necessary. Place the dates,
boiling water and bicarbonate of soda in a bowl, stir and
set aside for 10 minutes.

Lightly grease 4 metal pudding basins, 200 ml (7 fl oz)
each, and line the bases with nonstick baking paper.
Divide the golden syrup between the basins.

Place the margarine, sugar, flour, egg, vanilla and
ginger in a food processor and blend until smooth.
Drain the dates, add to the processor and blend briefly
to mix. Divide the mixture between the pudding basins,
cover the tops with greased foil and put in the slow
cooker pot.

Pour boiling water into the slow cooker pot to come
halfway up the sides of the basins, cover and cook on
High for 3½–4 hours until the sponge is well risen
and springs back when pressed with a fingertip.

Remove the foil, loosen the edges of the puddings
with a round-bladed knife and turn out into shallow
bowls. Peel away the lining paper and serve
immediately with the ice cream.

For sticky banana puddings, omit the dates, boiling
water and bicarbonate of soda. Follow the recipe above,
adding 1 ripe banana to the food processor with the
remaining ingredients. Blend and continue as above.
Calories per serving 411

index

acknowledgements

Senior Commissioning Editor: Eleanor Maxfield
Editor: Pollyanna Poulter
Design: Jeremy Tilston & Jaz Bahra
Production Controller: Sarah Kramer
Photographer: William Shaw

Photography copyright © Octopus Publishing Group/Stephen Conroy 6, 9, 10, 11, 13, 14, 15, 16, 27, 33, 35, 37, 39, 52, 55, 59, 69, 97, 99, 101, 103, 105, 147, 165, 167, 169, 171, 175, 209, 211, 213, 215, 217, 221, 223, 225, 227, 229, 233; Lis Parsons 118, 178; Ian Wallace 18.